Math Practice

Grades K-1

A Best Value Book™

Written by
Kelley Wingate Levy

Edited by
Aaron Levy

© Carson-Dellosa CD-3746

ISBN 0-88724-527-7

Table of Contents

Ready-To-Use Ideas and Activities

The only way children will truly be able to manipulate numbers and move on to higher level math concepts is to memorize the basic table and understand fundamental concepts, such as counting, addition, subtraction, time, and money.

The following pages will provide exercises to help reinforce basic skills using a variety of activities. These activities include a multi-sensory approach to helping children understand the concepts being introduced.

Take a bag of dried beans and put them in a bowl (any kind of dried bean can be used). Dried beans make great counters, and counters are extremely beneficial in helping children visualize mathematical concepts.

Show children some of the cut-apart flash cards provided in the back of this book, starting with the flash cards that use small numbers. On small pieces of paper write plus (+), minus (-), and equal (=) signs, to use with the flash cards. Put the flash cards on a table or on the floor. Use the beans and the paper signs to show what is on the flash card. For example:

use the beans to show 4 beans + 1 bean = 5 beans. Have the child state the problem and the answer out loud after the beans are in place. Children can also do this in small groups without an adult.

Use the beans to show examples of both addition and subtraction problems. After doing a number of examples using the flash cards, let the children make up their own problems and show them visually using the beans.

Ready-To-Use Ideas and Activities

Obtain a pair of dice and anything that will act as a three minute timer (a timer, stopwatch, or watch with a second hand), or decide upon a certain number of rounds of play. In turn, each child should roll the dice and add the two numbers together. (Each correct answer is worth one point.) The child with the most correct answers after a specific period of time or number of rounds wins. For example, one game may consist of six rolls of the dice. The child who has the most points after six rolls wins. Alternately, the game may be played by subtracting the smaller number from the larger.

As players memorize facts and gain confidence, add additional dice. When using more than two dice, the players should state the problem out loud and answer as they go. If, for instance, the dice show 3, 6, and 4, the player would say *3 plus 6 is 9 and 4 more is 13.*

Reproduce the bingo sheet included in this book, making enough to give one to each child. Write the flash card problems on a chalkboard. Have the students choose 24 different problems and write them in any order on the empty spaces of their bingo cards, writing only one problem in each space. When all students have finished filling out their bingo cards, take the flash cards and make them into a deck. Call out the answers one at a time. Any student who has a problem that equals the called out answer should make an "X" through the problem to cross it out (allow only one problem per answer). The student who first crosses out five problems in a row (horizontally, vertically, or diagonally) wins the game and shouts "BINGO!" Another fun version of this game is to write answers on the bingo sheet and call out the problems. To extend the game you can continue playing until a student crosses out all the problems on his bingo sheet.

B	I	N	G	O
		FREE		

Count the objects. Circle the correct number.

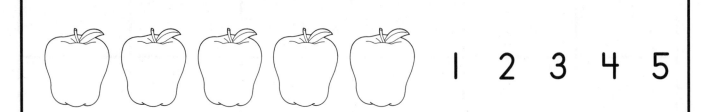

1   2   3   4   5

1   2   3   4   5

1   2   3   4   5

1   2   3   4   5

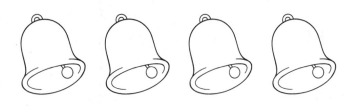

1   2   3   4   5

Draw a line to match each tree to the correct number of leaves.

Count the objects. Write the correct number in each blank.

_____

_____

_____

_____

_____

Count the objects. Circle the correct number.

6   7   8   9   10

6   7   8   9   10

6   7   8   9   10

6   7   8   9   10

6   7   8   9   10

Draw a line to match each backpack to the correct number of books.

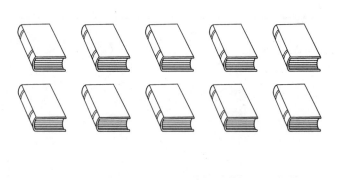

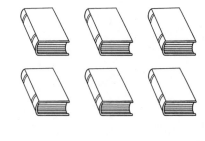

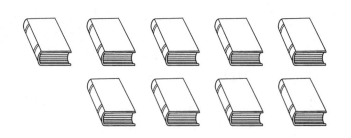

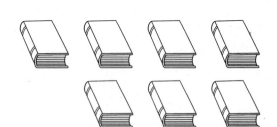

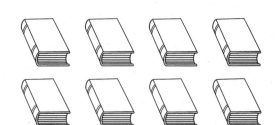

Count the objects. Write the correct number in each blank.

_____

_____

_____

_____

_____

Name _____

Count the objects. Circle the correct number.

11 12 13 14 15

11 12 13 14 15

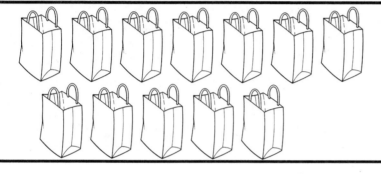

11 12 13 14 15

11 12 13 14 15

11 12 13 14 15

Draw a line to match each barn to the correct number of chicks.

Count the shapes. Write the correct number in each blank.

_____

_____

_____

_____

_____

Write the number that comes next.

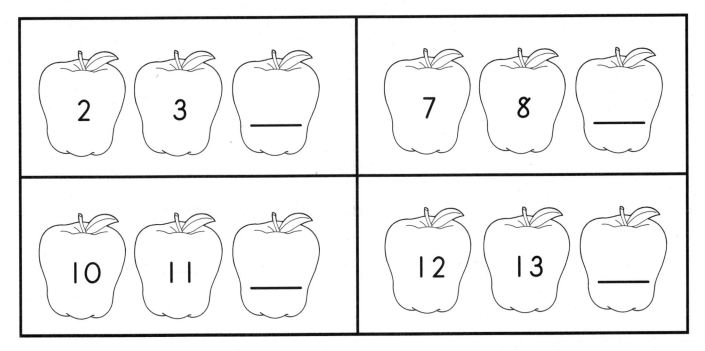

Write the number that comes first.

Write the number that comes between.

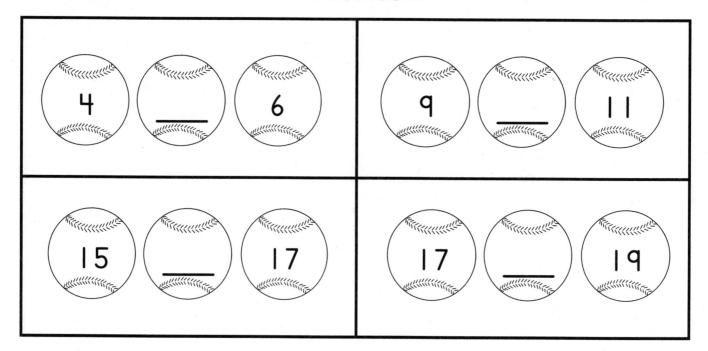

4 __ 6   9 __ 11

15 __ 17   17 __ 19

Write the correct number in the blank space.

6 __ 8   11 12 __

__ 13 14   18 __ 20

Circle the larger set in each box.

Name _____   Skill: Number of Objects in a Group

Circle the larger set in each box.

Name _____

Circle the smaller set in each box.

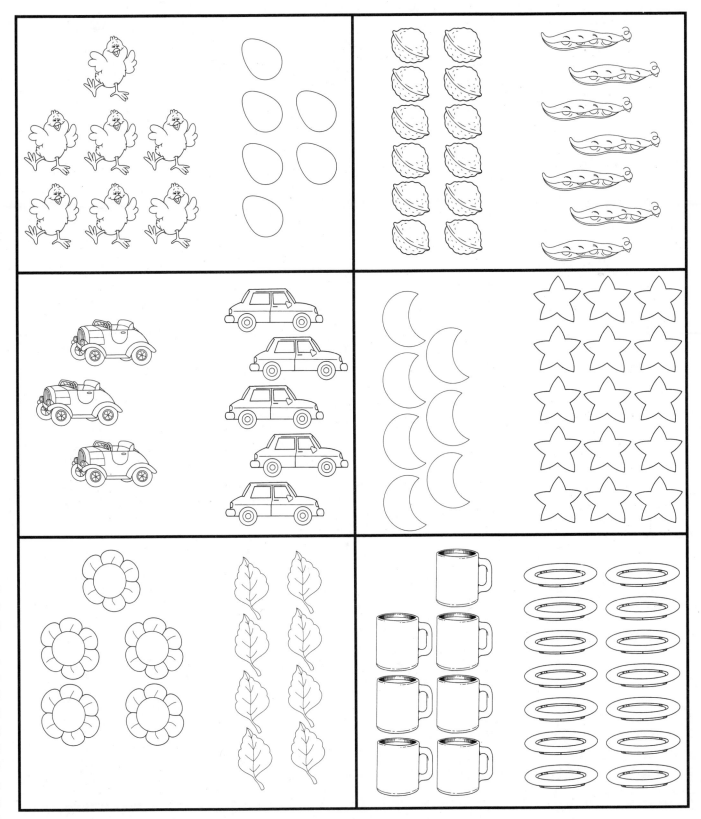

Name _____

Draw a line to match the sets with the same number of objects.

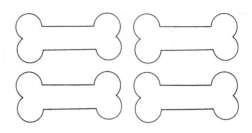

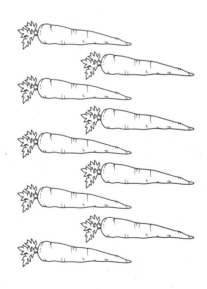

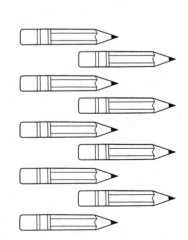

Name _____

Draw a line to match the sets with the same number of objects.

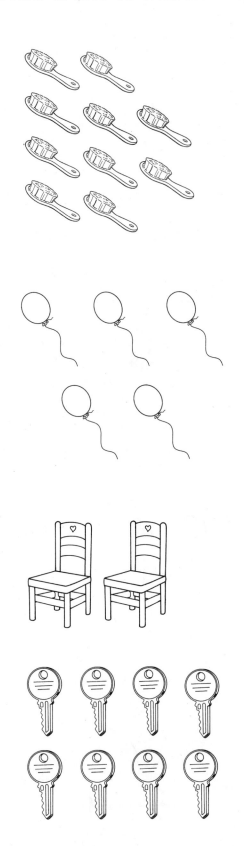

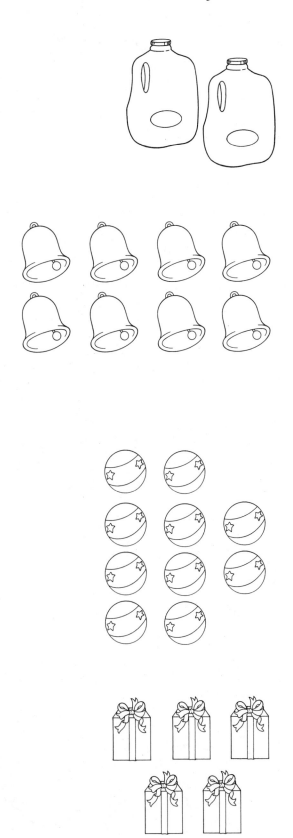

Circle the larger number in each cloud.

Circle the smaller number in each cloud.

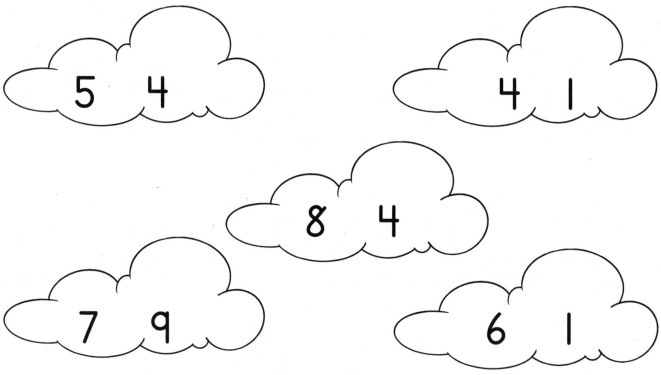

17

Name_____

Circle the correct number word.

1	one / four / zero	2	seven / two / six
3	nine / four / three	4	eight / five / four
5	five / ten / one	6	one / two / six
7	seven / zero / ten	8	eight / four / one
9	nine / three / six	10	two / ten / seven

Draw a line to match each number to its number word.

1 1   fifteen

1 2   thirteen

1 3   fourteen

1 4   eleven

1 5   twelve

Draw a line to match each number to its number word.

16   twenty

17   seventeen

18   sixteen

19   eighteen

20   nineteen

Name _____   Skill: Ordinal Numbers

Circle the ordinal number that names the position of each item below.

first   second   third   fourth   fifth   sixth   seventh   eighth   ninth   tenth

(banana)	sixth	seventh	first
(cherries)	second	fourth	tenth
(apple)	sixth	fifth	first
(egg)	ninth	second	eighth
(orange)	fourth	tenth	seventh
(pretzel)	eighth	fifth	sixth
(bread)	second	tenth	seventh
(tomato)	fourth	third	eighth
(cheese)	fifth	fourth	tenth
(cupcake)	eighth	second	sixth

Even numbers can be divided into 2 equal groups. Numbers that end in 0, 2, 4, 6, or 8 are even numbers. Circle the even numbers in each row.

2	3	4	6	10
1	2	8	12	14
11	12	13	19	21
16	17	19	20	22
18	23	25	26	28
24	26	27	29	30

In each blank, write the even number that would come next.

2, 4, 6, ___, 10, 12, ___, 16, ___

Odd numbers cannot be divided into 2 equal groups. Numbers that end in 1, 3, 5, 7, or 9 are odd numbers. Circle the odd numbers in each row.

1	3	4	6	10
5	6	7	9	11
12	14	15	17	20
13	16	18	19	21
17	18	20	22	23
24	26	27	29	30

In each blank, write the odd number that would come next.

1, 3, 5, ____, 9, 11, ____, 15, ____

Name _____

Use the number lines to skip count by 2s. On each row, begin
with the first even number. Place a dot on each number in the
series.

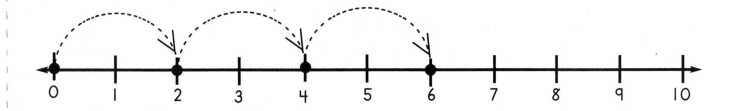

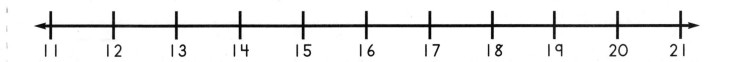

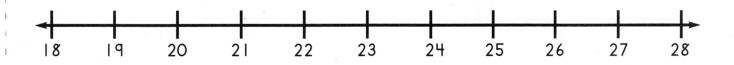

Fill in the blank squares. Skip count by 2s.

1		3		5
	7		9	
11		13		15
	17		19	

Write the next five even numbers to continue the pattern.

22 _____ _____ _____ _____

Complete the pattern. Skip count by 2s.

| 2 | 4 | ___ | ___ | 10 |

| 12 | ___ | 16 | ___ | 20 |

| ___ | 24 | ___ | 28 | ___ |

Name _____

Skill: Counting by Twos

Count by 2s to complete the grids below.

2		6	8	
12	14	16		20
		26	28	30

	4	6		10
12		16	18	
	24		28	

Use the number lines to count by 5s. Write the correct number in each box.

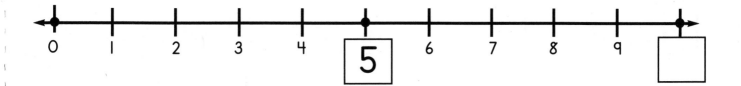

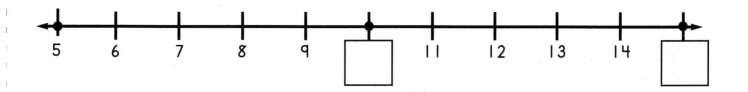

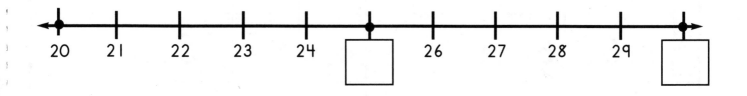

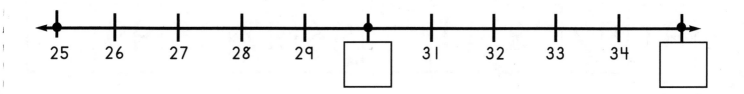

Name _____

Fill in the missing numbers. Skip count by 5s.

1	2	3	4		6	7	8	9	
11	12	13	14		16	17	18	19	
21	22	23	24		26	27	28	29	
31	32	33	34		36	37	38	39	
41	42	43	44		46	47	48	49	
51	52	53	54		56	57	58	59	
61	62	63	64		66	67	68	69	
71	72	73	74		76	77	78	79	
81	82	83	84		86	87	88	89	
91	92	93	94		96	97	98	99	

Name _____

Complete the pattern. Skip count by 5s.

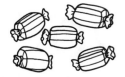 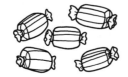 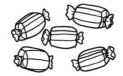 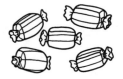

_____5_____   _____10_____   _____   _____20_____

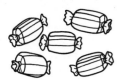 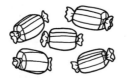  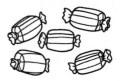

_____25_____   _____   _____35_____   _____

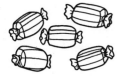  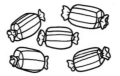 

_____45_____   _____   _____   _____60_____

Count by 5s. Fill in the blank squares.

5	10		20
25			
	50		
65			80
			100

Name _____   Skill: Counting by Tens

Use the number lines to count by 10s. Write the correct number in each box.

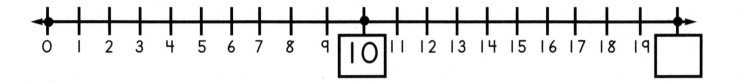

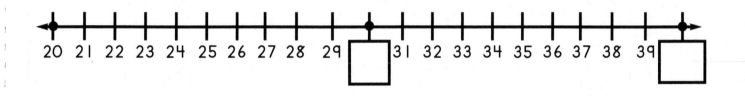

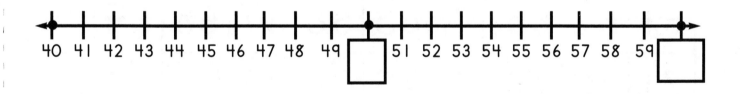

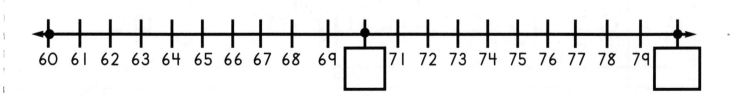

Name _____

Fill in the missing numbers. Skip count by 10s.

1	2	3	4	5	6	7	8	9	
11	12	13	14	15	16	17	18	19	
21	22	23	24	25	26	27	28	29	
31	32	33	34	35	36	37	38	39	
41	42	43	44	45	46	47	48	49	
51	52	53	54	55	56	57	58	59	
61	62	63	64	65	66	67	68	69	
71	72	73	74	75	76	77	78	79	
81	82	83	84	85	86	87	88	89	
91	92	93	94	95	96	97	98	99	

Complete the series. Skip count by 10s.

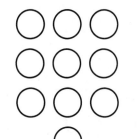

__10__

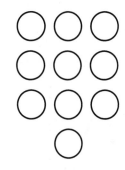

__20__

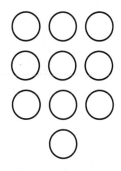

_____

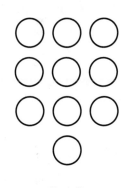

__40__

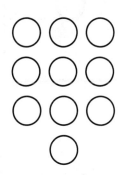

_____

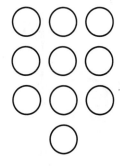

__60__

_____

_____

__80__

_____

_____

__110__

__120__

Count by 10s. Fill in the blank squares.

10	20			50
60		80		100

10		30	40	
	70		90	

Add.

1.   1
    + 5

2.   3
    + 3

3.   6
    + 0

4.   2
    + 3

5.   1
    + 0

6.   2
    + 0

7.   3
    + 2

8.   2
    + 2

9.   1
    + 1

10.   4
    + 1

11.   3
    + 1

12.   1
    + 3

13.   4
    + 0

14.   2
    + 4

15.   3
    + 3

Total Problems   15   Problems Correct _____

Add.

1.
2 + 3 =

2.
1 + 2 =

3.
4 + 2 =

4.
1 + 5 =

5.
4 + 0 =

6.
5 + 1 =

7.
4 + 2 =

8.
2 + 2 =

9.
4 + 1 =

10.
0 + 4 =

11.
3 + 2 =

12.
3 + 3 =

Total Problems __12__ Problems Correct _____

Add.

1. $\begin{array}{r} 1 \\ +\ 4 \\ \hline \end{array}$ 2. $\begin{array}{r} 4 \\ +\ 3 \\ \hline \end{array}$ 3. $\begin{array}{r} 6 \\ +\ 2 \\ \hline \end{array}$ 4. $\begin{array}{r} 5 \\ +\ 3 \\ \hline \end{array}$ 5. $\begin{array}{r} 1 \\ +\ 7 \\ \hline \end{array}$

6. $\begin{array}{r} 3 \\ +\ 4 \\ \hline \end{array}$ 7. $\begin{array}{r} 3 \\ +\ 5 \\ \hline \end{array}$ 8. $\begin{array}{r} 2 \\ +\ 0 \\ \hline \end{array}$ 9. $\begin{array}{r} 1 \\ +\ 3 \\ \hline \end{array}$ 10. $\begin{array}{r} 4 \\ +\ 4 \\ \hline \end{array}$

11. $\begin{array}{r} 6 \\ +\ 1 \\ \hline \end{array}$ 12. $\begin{array}{r} 1 \\ +\ 5 \\ \hline \end{array}$ 13. $\begin{array}{r} 2 \\ +\ 0 \\ \hline \end{array}$ 14. $\begin{array}{r} 2 \\ +\ 6 \\ \hline \end{array}$ 15. $\begin{array}{r} 2 \\ +\ 4 \\ \hline \end{array}$

Total Problems 15   Problems Correct _____

Add.

1. 2
   + 4

2. 4
   + 4

3. 6
   + 1

4. 5
   + 0

5. 1
   + 6

6. 3
   + 2

7. 3
   + 4

8. 2
   + 6

9. 4
   + 3

10. 4
    + 4

11. 6
    + 2

12. 1
    + 3

13. 2
    + 3

14. 2
    + 1

15. 3
    + 4

Total Problems 15   Problems Correct _____

Add.

1.   7   2.   8   3.   0   4.   9   5.   2
     + 2   + 0   + 10   + 0   + 6

6.   3   7.   1   8.   0   9.   1   10.   7
     + 7   + 9   + 7   + 8   + 3

11.   3   12.   1   13.   7   14.   5   15.   6
     + 4   + 7   + 0   + 4   + 3

Total Problems 15   Problems Correct _____

Add.

1. $5 + 1 =$

2. $8 + 1 =$

3. $9 + 0 =$

4. $4 + 1 =$

5. $4 + 2 =$

6. $5 + 3 =$

7. $3 + 2 =$

8. $3 + 7 =$

9. $6 + 2 =$

10. $6 + 3 =$

11. $5 + 4 =$

12. $3 + 4 =$

13. $4 + 6 =$

14. $7 + 3 =$

15. $2 + 7 =$

Total Problems 15   Problems Correct _____

Add.

1.   5
   + 4

2.   7
   + 3

3.   6
   + 4

4.   5
   + 2

5.   4
   + 7

6.   3
   + 5

7.   6
   + 5

8.   2
   + 9

9.   2
   + 6

10.   8
    + 3

11.   4
    + 4

12.   3
    + 6

13. 10
    + 1

14. 11
    + 0

15.   5
    + 4

Total Problems __15__   Problems Correct _____

Name _____

Add.

1. 9
   + 2

2. 11
   + 0

3. 10
   + 1

4. 9
   + 0

5. 5
   + 6

6. 3
   + 6

7. 1
   + 9

8. 4
   + 7

9. 2
   + 8

10. 7
   + 4

11. 3
   + 5

12. 3
   + 7

13. 0
   + 8

14. 6
   + 4

15. 6
   + 5

Total Problems 15   Problems Correct _____

43

Name _____

Add.

1.   7
   + 5

2.   8
   + 3

3.   10
   + 2

4.   9
   + 2

5.   6
   + 6

6.   4
   + 7

7.   10
   + 1

8.   3
   + 7

9.   1
   + 9

10.   7
   + 3

11.   3
   + 6

12.   5
   + 7

13.   7
   + 5

14.   5
   + 3

15.   7
   + 3

Total Problems __15__ Problems Correct _____

Add.

1. $\begin{array}{r} 7 \\ + 4 \\ \hline \end{array}$ 2. $\begin{array}{r} 12 \\ + 0 \\ \hline \end{array}$ 3. $\begin{array}{r} 10 \\ + 2 \\ \hline \end{array}$ 4. $\begin{array}{r} 9 \\ + 3 \\ \hline \end{array}$ 5. $\begin{array}{r} 4 \\ + 6 \\ \hline \end{array}$

6. $\begin{array}{r} 3 \\ + 6 \\ \hline \end{array}$ 7. $\begin{array}{r} 1 \\ + 8 \\ \hline \end{array}$ 8. $\begin{array}{r} 2 \\ + 7 \\ \hline \end{array}$ 9. $\begin{array}{r} 4 \\ + 8 \\ \hline \end{array}$ 10. $\begin{array}{r} 7 \\ + 5 \\ \hline \end{array}$

11. $\begin{array}{r} 3 \\ + 5 \\ \hline \end{array}$ 12. $\begin{array}{r} 3 \\ + 7 \\ \hline \end{array}$ 13. $\begin{array}{r} 7 \\ + 1 \\ \hline \end{array}$ 14. $\begin{array}{r} 5 \\ + 6 \\ \hline \end{array}$ 15. $\begin{array}{r} 6 \\ + 4 \\ \hline \end{array}$

Total Problems __15__   Problems Correct _____

Add.

1. 7 + 6	**2.** 8 + 5	**3.** 10 + 2	**4.** 9 + 3	**5.** 5 + 6
6. 4 + 7	**7.** 2 + 9	**8.** 5 + 7	**9.** 3 + 8	**10.** 7 + 4
11. 8 + 3	**12.** 3 + 6	**13.** 7 + 6	**14.** 8 + 5	**15.** 6 + 6

Total Problems __15__ Problems Correct _____

Add.

1.   5
   + 7

2.   9
   + 2

3.   10
   + 3

4.   9
   + 4

5.   2
   + 5

6.   5
   + 5

7.   2
   + 9

8.   6
   + 7

9.   4
   + 8

10.   7
   + 1

11.   3
   + 9

12.   3
   + 7

13.   7
   + 2

14.   5
   + 4

15.   7
   + 3

Total Problems _15_ **Problems Correct** _____

Skill: Sums to Fourteen

Add.

1. 7 + 6	**2.** 8 + 5	**3.** 6 + 2	**4.** 9 + 4	**5.** 6 + 6
6. 6 + 7	**7.** 2 + 9	**8.** 7 + 7	**9.** 6 + 8	**10.** 7 + 7
11. 6 + 6	**12.** 5 + 7	**13.** 7 + 4	**14.** 5 + 3	**15.** 6 + 4

Total Problems __15__ Problems Correct _____

Name _____

Add.

1.   7
   + 5
	2. 8
	   + 3
		3. 10
		   + 4
			4. 9
			   + 3
				5. 6
				   + 6

6.   5
   + 7
	7. 5
	   + 9
		8. 7
		   + 7
			9. 3
			   + 8
				10. 7
				   + 7

11.   3
   + 9
	12. 3
	   + 7
		13. 6
		   + 8
			14. 5
			   + 7
				15. 6
				   + 5

Total Problems   15   Problems Correct _____

Name _____   Skill: Sums to Fifteen

Add.

1. 7   2. 8   3. 10   4. 9   5. 3
  + 8   + 7   + 5   + 6   + 6

6. 6   7. 4   8. 5   9. 3   10. 7
  + 7   + 9   + 7   + 8   + 5

11. 4   12. 5   13. 7   14. 5   15. 6
   + 9   + 7   + 6   + 6   + 7

Total Problems __15__   Problems Correct _____

© Carson-Dellosa CD-3746   50

Add.

1. 8
   + 7

2. 6
   + 9

3. 10
   + 1

4. 9
   + 3

5. 1
   + 6

6. 5
   + 7

7. 2
   + 9

8. 7
   + 7

9. 2
   + 8

10. 7
    + 4

11. 6
    + 4

12. 3
    + 7

13. 7
    + 2

14. 5
    + 6

15. 6
    + 5

Total Problems __15__   Problems Correct _____

51

Add.

1. 9
    + 4

2. 8
    + 7

3. 10
    + 6

4. 10
    + 2

5. 7
    + 9

6. 10
    + 5

7. 6
    + 9

8. 11
    + 4

9. 8
    + 8

10. 9
     + 6

11. 8
     + 5

12. 7
     + 7

13. 7
     + 6

14. 5
     + 9

15. 6
     + 4

Total Problems 15 Problems Correct _____

Add.

1.   9
  + 5

2.   12
  + 4

3.   11
  + 4

4.   10
  + 6

5.   9
  + 3

6.   8
  + 7

7.   5
  + 5

8.   13
  + 2

9.   6
  + 7

10.   2
  + 8

11.   7
  + 9

12.   6
  + 8

13.   4
  + 2

14.   5
  + 6

15.   9
  + 4

Total Problems 15   Problems Correct _____

Name _____

Add.

| 1. | 5
 + 7 | 2. | 15
 + 1 | 3. | 14
 + 3 | 4. | 11
 + 4 | 5. | 9
 + 8 |

| 6. | 4
 + 7 | 7. | 5
 + 8 | 8. | 8
 + 9 | 9. | 13
 + 3 | 10. | 14
 + 3 |

| 11. | 9
 + 4 | 12. | 6
 + 4 | 13. | 3
 + 8 | 14. | 5
 + 9 | 15. | 10
 + 7 |

Total Problems __15__   Problems Correct _____

Add.

1.   10
   + 7

2.   13
   + 4

3.   11
   + 4

4.   12
   + 5

5.   7
   + 9

6.   10
   + 3

7.   15
   + 1

8.   9
   + 4

9.   7
   + 6

10. 10
   + 5

11.   7
   + 7

12.   8
   + 7

13. 11
   + 6

14.   6
   + 3

15.   9
   + 5

Total Problems 15   Problems Correct _____

Name _____

Add.

1. 8
     + 7

2. 6
     + 9

3. 10
     + 8

4. 10
     + 2

5. 12
     + 5

6. 13
     + 4

7. 11
     + 5

8. 9
     + 5

9. 10
     + 4

10. 9
      + 2

11. 4
      + 9

12. 12
      + 1

13. 4
      + 7

14. 14
      + 4

15. 15
      + 2

Total Problems 15   Problems Correct _____

Name _____   Skill: Sums to Eighteen

Add.

1. 15   2. 12   3. 11   4.   8   5.   7
   + 3   + 4   + 2   + 2   + 6

6. 10   7.   8   8. 11   9. 13   10.   9
   + 5   + 9   + 7   + 5   + 7

11. 10   12.   9   13. 12   14.   9   15.   8
   + 8   + 3   + 5   + 9   + 5

Total Problems 15   Problems Correct _____

57

Name _____   Skill: Subtracting from Six or Less

Subtract.

1.   5
    – 5

2.   3
    – 3

3.   6
    – 0

4.   6
    – 3

5.   1
    – 0

6.   2
    – 0

7.   3
    – 2

8.   2
    – 2

9.   1
    – 1

10.   4
    – 1

11.   3
    – 1

12.   5
    – 3

13.   4
    – 0

14.   5
    – 4

15.   3
    – 3

Total Problems _15_   Problems Correct _____

58

Name _____   Skill: Subtracting from Six or Less

Subtract.

1. 6
   − 3

2. 4
   − 0

3. 3
   − 3

4. 5
   − 2

5. 6
   − 2

6. 2
   − 2

7. 4
   − 2

8. 3
   − 2

9. 6
   − 4

10. 4
    − 3

11. 1
    − 1

12. 3
    − 0

13. 4
    − 1

14. 3
    − 1

15. 5
    − 1

Total Problems 15   Problems Correct _____

Subtract.

1. $\begin{array}{r} 6 \\ -3 \\ \hline \end{array}$
2. $\begin{array}{r} 10 \\ -6 \\ \hline \end{array}$
3. $\begin{array}{r} 7 \\ -5 \\ \hline \end{array}$
4. $\begin{array}{r} 10 \\ -8 \\ \hline \end{array}$
5. $\begin{array}{r} 8 \\ -4 \\ \hline \end{array}$

6. $\begin{array}{r} 9 \\ -4 \\ \hline \end{array}$
7. $\begin{array}{r} 7 \\ -3 \\ \hline \end{array}$
8. $\begin{array}{r} 6 \\ -4 \\ \hline \end{array}$
9. $\begin{array}{r} 9 \\ -5 \\ \hline \end{array}$
10. $\begin{array}{r} 10 \\ -3 \\ \hline \end{array}$

11. $\begin{array}{r} 8 \\ -6 \\ \hline \end{array}$
12. $\begin{array}{r} 9 \\ -3 \\ \hline \end{array}$
13. $\begin{array}{r} 10 \\ -1 \\ \hline \end{array}$
14. $\begin{array}{r} 7 \\ -6 \\ \hline \end{array}$
15. $\begin{array}{r} 8 \\ -2 \\ \hline \end{array}$

Total Problems 15   Problems Correct _____

Subtract.

1.   9
   − 2

2.   7
   − 5

3.   10
   − 3

4.   10
   − 5

5.   6
   − 4

6.   8
   − 6

7.   7
   − 2

8.   9
   − 7

9.   3
   − 2

10.   8
   − 2

11.   10
   − 4

12.   9
   − 8

13.   9
   − 5

14.   8
   − 3

15.   7
   − 3

Total Problems _15_ Problems Correct _____

Name _____   Skill: Subtracting from Eleven or Less

Subtract.

1. 9
  − 3

2. 10
  − 6

3. 7
  − 5

4. 9
  − 8

5. 8
  − 4

6. 9
  − 4

7. 11
  − 2

8. 6
  − 4

9. 9
  − 5

10. 11
  − 3

11. 8
  − 8

12. 7
  − 3

13. 11
  − 1

14. 11
  − 6

15. 11
  − 2

Total Problems __15__   Problems Correct _____

Subtract.

1. 10
   − 6

2. 11
   − 3

3.   6
   − 5

4. 11
   − 8

5. 10
   − 4

6. 10
   − 8

7.   6
   − 3

8. 10
   − 4

9.   8
   − 3

10. 11
   − 5

11. 9
   − 6

12. 11
   − 6

13. 8
   − 4

14. 6
   − 2

15. 9
   − 1

Total Problems 15   Problems Correct _____

Name _____   Skill: Subtracting from Twelve or Less

Subtract.

1. $\begin{array}{r} 12 \\ -\ 3 \\ \hline \end{array}$
2. $\begin{array}{r} 11 \\ -\ 6 \\ \hline \end{array}$
3. $\begin{array}{r} 10 \\ -\ 5 \\ \hline \end{array}$
4. $\begin{array}{r} 12 \\ -\ 8 \\ \hline \end{array}$
5. $\begin{array}{r} 12 \\ -\ 4 \\ \hline \end{array}$

6. $\begin{array}{r} 9 \\ -\ 2 \\ \hline \end{array}$
7. $\begin{array}{r} 9 \\ -\ 5 \\ \hline \end{array}$
8. $\begin{array}{r} 11 \\ -\ 4 \\ \hline \end{array}$
9. $\begin{array}{r} 10 \\ -\ 4 \\ \hline \end{array}$
10. $\begin{array}{r} 12 \\ -\ 5 \\ \hline \end{array}$

11. $\begin{array}{r} 11 \\ -\ 6 \\ \hline \end{array}$
12. $\begin{array}{r} 9 \\ -\ 4 \\ \hline \end{array}$
13. $\begin{array}{r} 11 \\ -\ 1 \\ \hline \end{array}$
14. $\begin{array}{r} 9 \\ -\ 6 \\ \hline \end{array}$
15. $\begin{array}{r} 8 \\ -\ 3 \\ \hline \end{array}$

Total Problems 15   Problems Correct _____

Name _____

Subtract.

1. 11
    − 2

2. 12
    − 5

3. 9
    − 2

4. 8
    − 6

5. 9
    − 3

6. 9
    − 8

7. 12
    − 8

8. 11
    − 7

9. 12
    − 2

10. 7
    − 2

11. 10
    − 5

12. 9
    − 6

13. 12
    − 3

14. 7
    − 4

15. 9
    − 5

Total Problems __15__   Problems Correct _____

Subtract.

1. 13
    − 3

2. 13
    − 6

3. 9
    − 5

4. 10
    − 5

5. 8
    − 1

6. 12
    − 4

7. 10
    − 3

8. 9
    − 4

9. 8
    − 5

10. 11
    − 3

11. 12
    − 6

12. 8
    − 3

13. 13
    − 5

14. 10
    − 6

15. 9
    − 3

Total Problems 15 Problems Correct _____

Name _____

Subtract.

1.　13
　　− 5

2.　　9
　　− 3

3.　10
　　− 3

4.　11
　　− 8

5.　　9
　　− 4

6.　　9
　　− 6

7.　　9
　　− 3

8.　13
　　− 7

9.　　7
　　− 3

10.　3
　　− 2

11.　10
　　− 4

12.　13
　　− 6

13.　9
　　− 4

14.　8
　　− 2

15.　9
　　− 2

┌───┐
│ **Total Problems _15_ Problems Correct _____** │
└───┘

Subtract.

1. 14
    − 3

2. 14
    − 6

3. 10
    − 2

4. 10
    − 5

5. 11
    − 6

6. 12
    − 5

7. 13
    − 1

8. 14
    − 7

9. 12
    − 8

10. 11
    − 9

11. 12
    − 3

12. 14
    − 5

13. 10
    − 8

14. 10
    − 7

15. 9
    − 2

Total Problems 15   Problems Correct _____

68

Subtract.

1. 13
    − 5

2. 11
    − 8

3. 9
    − 3

4. 12
    − 4

5. 14
    − 7

6. 13
    − 8

7. 10
    − 6

8. 11
    − 5

9. 12
    − 9

10. 10
    − 8

11. 14
    − 2

12. 10
    − 4

13. 9
    − 5

14. 11
    − 7

15. 14
    − 6

Total Problems _15_ Problems Correct _____

Name _____   Skill: Subtracting from Fifteen or Less

Subtract.

1. 13
   – 3

2. 14
   – 6

3. 15
   – 5

4. 11
   – 5

5. 10
   – 1

6. 12
   – 4

7. 10
   – 3

8. 14
   – 4

9. 15
   – 2

10. 11
    – 3

11. 12
    – 6

12. 15
    – 8

13. 10
    – 5

14. 11
    – 6

15. 15
    – 3

Total Problems _15_   Problems Correct _____

Name _____   Skill: Subtracting from Fifteen or Less

Subtract.

1. 13   2. 15   3. 12   4. 10   5. 11
   - 6   - 3   - 8   - 8   - 5

6. 15   7. 10   8. 13   9. 12   10. 15
   - 6   - 3   - 5   - 3   - 2

11. 13   12. 14   13. 15   14. 11   15. 10
    - 4   - 6   - 9   - 2   - 2

Total Problems 15   Problems Correct _____

© Carson-Dellosa CD-3746   71

Subtract.

1. 13
   − 2

2. 12
   − 8

3. 10
   − 7

4. 11
   − 9

5. 16
   − 5

6. 13
   − 8

7. 10
   − 6

8. 12
   − 2

9. 10
   − 8

10. 16
   − 4

11. 15
   − 6

12. 16
   − 9

13. 11
   − 5

14. 12
   − 3

15. 13
   − 3

Total Problems 15   Problems Correct _____

Name _____   Skill: Subtracting from Sixteen or Less

Subtract.

1. 16 − 5	**2.** 13 − 3	**3.** 15 − 3	**4.** 12 − 8	**5.** 14 − 4
6. 12 − 6	**7.** 15 − 3	**8.** 14 − 7	**9.** 16 − 3	**10.** 13 − 2
11. 14 − 4	**12.** 12 − 6	**13.** 16 − 4	**14.** 13 − 2	**15.** 15 − 2

Total Problems 15   Problems Correct _____

Name _____   Skill: Subtracting from Seventeen or Less

Subtract.

1. 17 − 6	**2.** 15 − 3	**3.** 13 − 8	**4.** 17 − 5	**5.** 16 − 1
6. 14 − 4	**7.** 10 − 3	**8.** 15 − 4	**9.** 13 − 9	**10.** 14 − 3
11. 12 − 6	**12.** 17 − 6	**13.** 16 − 5	**14.** 15 − 4	**15.** 11 − 3

Total Problems 15   Problems Correct _____

Name _____ Skill: Subtracting from Seventeen or Less

Subtract.

1.   17
   − 5

2.   12
   − 8

3.   16
   − 5

4.   15
   − 2

5.   14
   − 4

6.   12
   − 4

7.   13
   − 3

8.   17
   − 6

9.   15
   − 9

10.   14
   − 2

11.   17
   − 5

12.   15
   − 4

13.   13
   − 7

14.   17
   − 7

15.   11
   − 8

Total Problems 15   Problems Correct _____

Name _____   Skill: Subtracting from Eighteen or Less

Subtract.

1. 18   **2.** 14   **3.** 16   **4.** 10   **5.** 15
   − 3   − 4   − 5   − 6   − 7

6. 12   **7.** 14   **8.** 18   **9.** 11   **10.** 16
   − 7   − 8   − 9   − 3   − 9

11. 13   **12.** 12   **13.** 10   **14.** 18   **15.** 17
   − 4   − 5   − 2   − 7   − 3

Total Problems __15__   Problems Correct _____

© Carson-Dellosa CD-3746   76

Subtract.

1.   17
    − 4

2.   9
    − 5

3.   14
    − 2

4.   18
    − 2

5.   16
    − 5

6.   14
    − 3

7.   18
    − 1

8.   16
    − 4

9.   17
    − 6

10.   15
    − 7

11.   17
    − 8

12.   10
    − 3

13.   12
    − 2

14.   15
    − 6

15.   18
    − 2

Total Problems __15__   **Problems Correct** _____

Name _____   Skill: Addition and Subtraction through Ten

Add or subtract.

1. 8
   − 5

2. 7
   + 2

3. 9
   − 3

4. 4
   + 3

5. 5
   − 2

6. 8
   + 2

7. 7
   + 3

8. 10
   − 6

9. 2
   − 2

10. 9
    + 1

11. 6
    − 6

12. 8
    + 0

13. 9
    + 0

14. 2
    + 3

15. 10
    − 6

┌───┐
│   **Total Problems 15   Problems Correct** _____ │
└───┘

78

Name _____   Skill: Addition and Subtraction through Ten

Add or subtract.

1.   9
    − 3

2.   8
    + 1

3.   5
    − 2

4.   7
    + 1

5.   8
    − 3

6.   9
    + 1

7.   10
    + 0

8.   10
    − 2

9.   7
    − 5

10.   6
    + 2

11.   5
    − 3

12.   9
    + 1

13.   7
    + 0

14.   2
    + 2

15.   9
    − 6

Total Problems 15   Problems Correct _____

Name _____   Skill: Addition and Subtraction through Ten

Add or subtract.

1. $\begin{array}{r} 6 \\ -2 \\ \hline \end{array}$	**2.** $\begin{array}{r} 9 \\ +1 \\ \hline \end{array}$	**3.** $\begin{array}{r} 5 \\ -3 \\ \hline \end{array}$	**4.** $\begin{array}{r} 8 \\ +1 \\ \hline \end{array}$	**5.** $\begin{array}{r} 8 \\ -2 \\ \hline \end{array}$
6. $\begin{array}{r} 8 \\ +2 \\ \hline \end{array}$	**7.** $\begin{array}{r} 9 \\ +0 \\ \hline \end{array}$	**8.** $\begin{array}{r} 8 \\ -3 \\ \hline \end{array}$	**9.** $\begin{array}{r} 9 \\ -6 \\ \hline \end{array}$	**10.** $\begin{array}{r} 3 \\ +2 \\ \hline \end{array}$
11. $\begin{array}{r} 5 \\ -2 \\ \hline \end{array}$	**12.** $\begin{array}{r} 8 \\ +1 \\ \hline \end{array}$	**13.** $\begin{array}{r} 7 \\ +1 \\ \hline \end{array}$	**14.** $\begin{array}{r} 4 \\ +2 \\ \hline \end{array}$	**15.** $\begin{array}{r} 9 \\ -5 \\ \hline \end{array}$

Total Problems __15__   Problems Correct _____

Name _____

Add.

1. 3
   + 1

2. 5
   + 4

3. 2
   + 7

4. 7
   + 1

5. 5
   + 2

6. 7
   + 0

7. 3
   + 6

8. 8
   + 1

9. 8
   + 0

10. 4
    + 3

11. 6
    + 1

12. 4
    + 4

13. 5
    + 3

14. 6
    + 2

15. 5
    + 3

Total Problems _15_   Problems Correct _____

81

Add.

1.   9
  + 9

2.   5
  + 6

3.   2
  + 8

4.   7
  + 6

5.   5
  + 6

6.   7
  + 8

7.   3
  + 9

8.   8
  + 5

9.   8
  + 8

10.   4
  + 7

11.   6
  + 8

12.   4
  + 7

13.   9
  + 8

14.   6
  + 7

15.   5
  + 6

Total Problems 15   Problems Correct _____

Name _____

Add.

1. 11
    + 8

2. 12
    + 3

3. 15
    + 4

4. 10
    + 7

5. 14
    + 4

6. 12
    + 7

7. 10
    + 5

8. 11
    + 6

9. 10
    + 2

10. 12
     + 1

11. 17
     + 1

12. 15
     + 2

13. 13
     + 5

14. 16
     + 2

15. 14
     + 3

Total Problems _15_ Problems Correct _____

Name _____

Add.

1.   11
    + 9

2.   15
    + 6

3.   19
    + 7

4.   16
    + 6

5.   17
    + 6

6.   14
    + 8

7.   13
    + 9

8.   16
    + 5

9.   12
    + 8

10.   15
    + 7

11.   15
    + 8

12.   17
    + 4

13.   14
    + 8

14.   13
    + 7

15.   18
    + 6

Total Problems 15   Problems Correct _____

Write the correct time in each blank.

__ __ : __ __   __ __ : __ __   __ __ : __ __

__ __ : __ __   __ __ : __ __   __ __ : __ __

Name _____   Skill: Telling Time on the Hour

Write the correct time in each blank.

__ __ : __ __   __ __ : __ __   __ __ : __ __

__ __ : __ __   __ __ : __ __   __ __ : __ __

86

Write the correct time in each blank.

___ : ___ ___   ___ : ___ ___   ___ ___ : ___ ___

___ : ___ ___   ___ : ___ ___   ___ : ___ ___

Write the correct time in each blank.

___:___ ___

___:___ ___

___:___ ___

___ ___:___ ___

___ ___:___ ___

___ ___:___ ___

Draw hands on each clock to show the correct time.

9:00

12:00

4:00

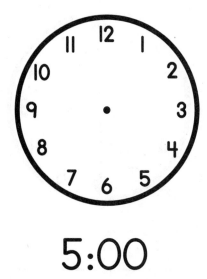

5:00

11:00

7:00

Name _____   Skill: Telling Time on the Half Hour

Draw hands on each clock to show the correct time.

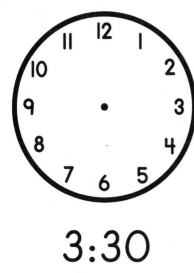

3:30

12:30

7:30

11:30

10:30

9:30

Draw a line to match the coin to the correct amount.

10¢

25¢

5¢

50¢

1¢

Name _____   Skill: Money

Draw a line to match the coin to the correct amount.

   50¢

   5¢

                                    1¢

   10¢

   25¢

© Carson-Dellosa CD-3746   92

Circle the correct amount in each box.

1¢   5¢   10¢

25¢   50¢

1¢   5¢   10¢

25¢   50¢

1¢   5¢   10¢

25¢   50¢

1¢   5¢   10¢

25¢   50¢

1¢   5¢   10¢

25¢   50¢

1¢   5¢   10¢

25¢   50¢

Name _____   Skill: Money

Draw a line to match each group of coins to the correct amount.

                           11¢

    15¢

    6¢

   26¢

    35¢

94

Name _____   Skill: Money

Draw a line to match each group of coins to the correct amount.

    30¢

    60¢

    51¢

    20¢

    55¢

Skill: Money

In each box, circle the group that has the larger amount.

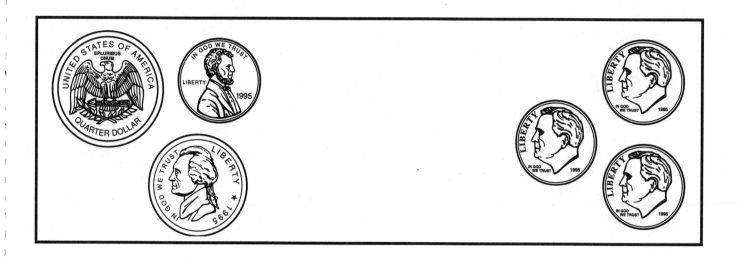

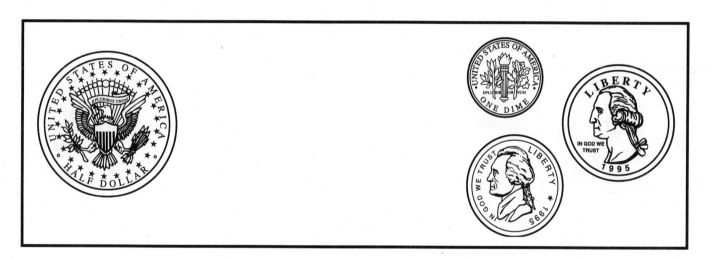

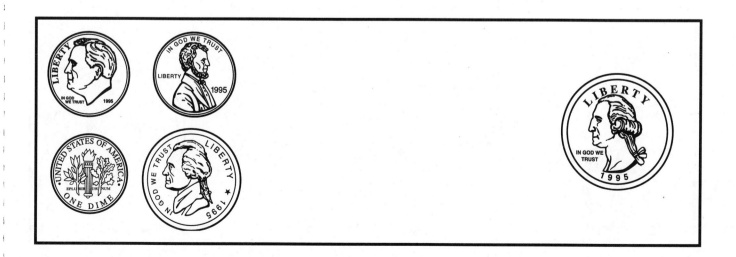

Name _____   Skill: Money

In each box, circle the group that has the smaller amount.

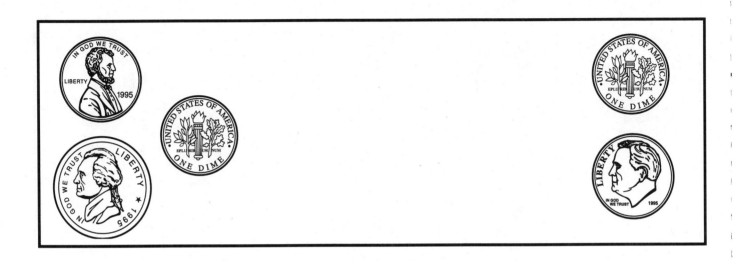

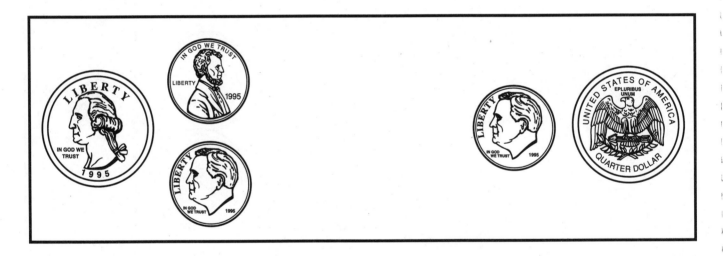

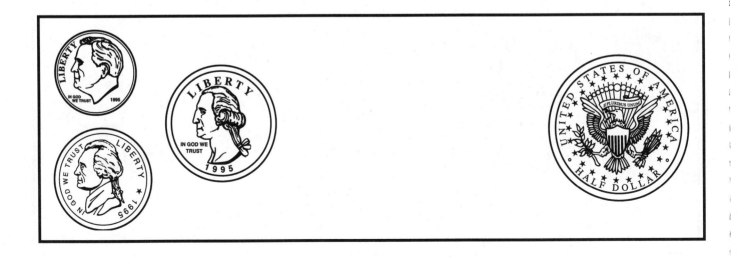

In each box, write the correct amount in the blank.

_____

_____

_____

_____

_____

_____

Answer Key

Name _____   Skill: Counting 0–5

Count the objects. Circle the correct number.

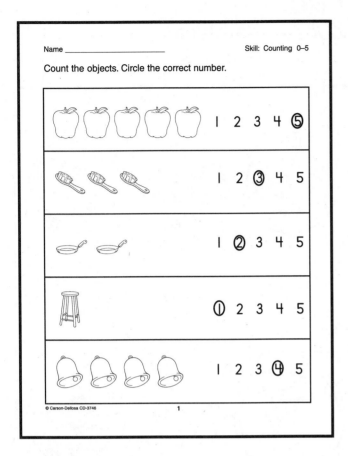

Name _____   Skill: Counting 0–5

Draw a line to match each tree to the correct number of leaves.

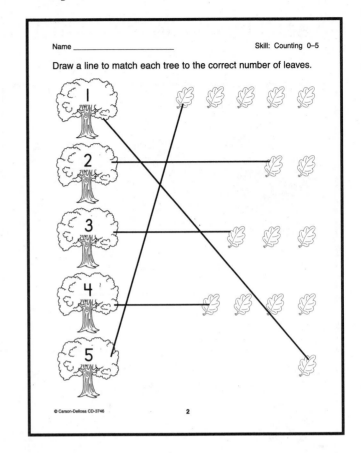

Name _____   Skill: Counting 0–5

Count the objects. Write the correct number in each blank.

Name _____   Skill: Counting 6–10

Count the objects. Circle the correct number.

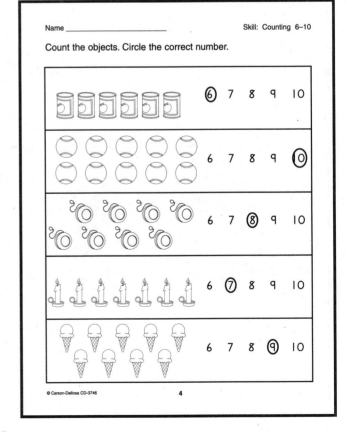

99

Answer Key

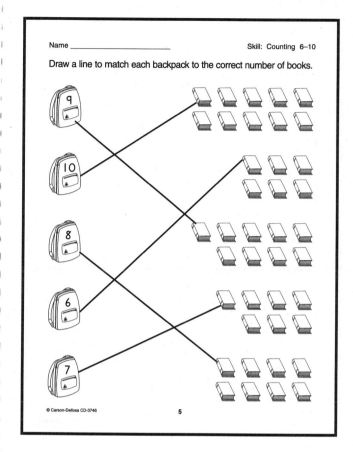

Name _____   Skill: Counting 6–10

Draw a line to match each backpack to the correct number of books.

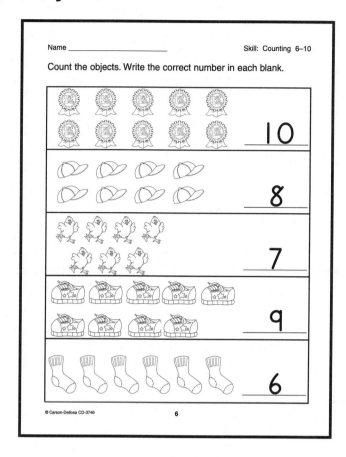

Name _____   Skill: Counting 6–10

Count the objects. Write the correct number in each blank.

10
8
7
9
6

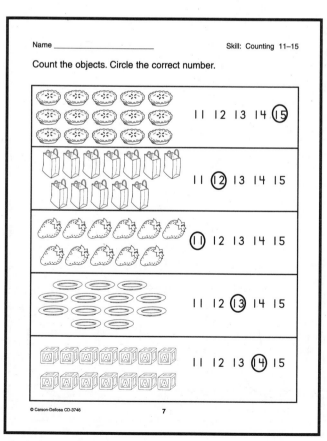

Name _____   Skill: Counting 11–15

Count the objects. Circle the correct number.

11 12 13 14 (15)
11 (12) 13 14 15
(11) 12 13 14 15
11 12 (13) 14 15
11 12 13 (14) 15

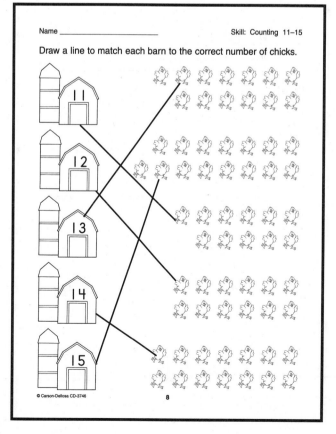

Name _____   Skill: Counting 11–15

Draw a line to match each barn to the correct number of chicks.

Answer Key

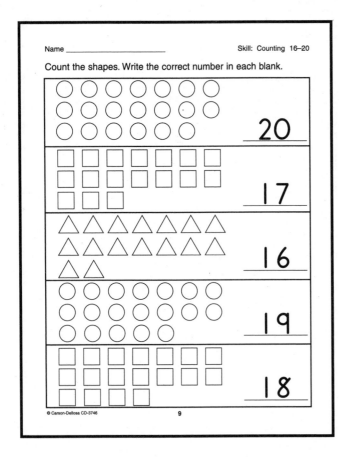

Name _____   Skill: Counting 16–20

Count the shapes. Write the correct number in each blank.

20

17

16

19

18

9

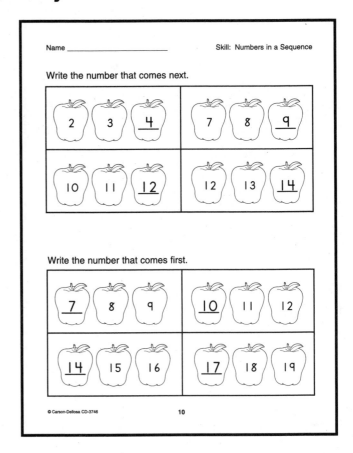

Name _____   Skill: Numbers in a Sequence

Write the number that comes next.

2   3   4   7   8   9

10   11   12   12   13   14

Write the number that comes first.

7   8   9   10   11   12

14   15   16   17   18   19

10

Name _____   Skill: Numbers in a Sequence

Write the number that comes between.

4   5   6   9   10   11

15   16   17   17   18   19

Write the correct number in the blank space.

6   7   8   11   12   13

12   13   14   18   19   20

11

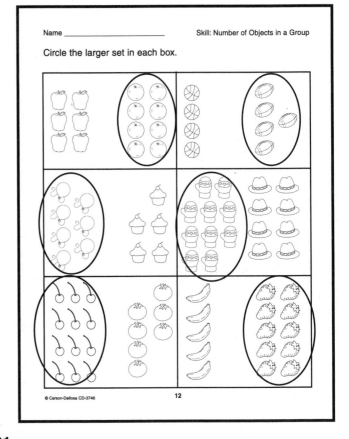

Name _____   Skill: Number of Objects in a Group

Circle the larger set in each box.

12

Answer Key

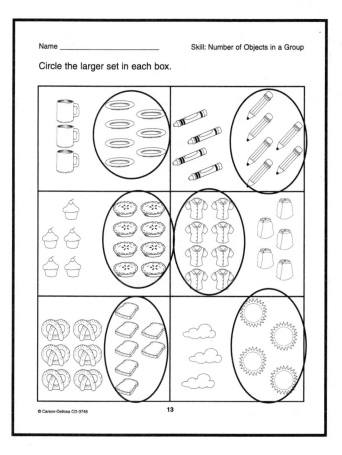

13

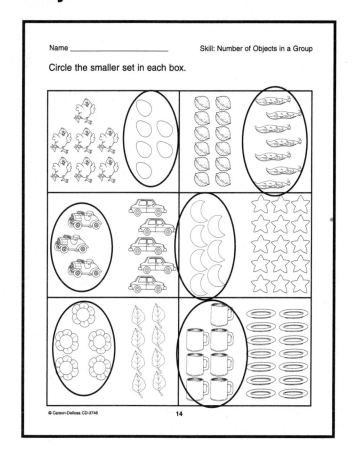

14

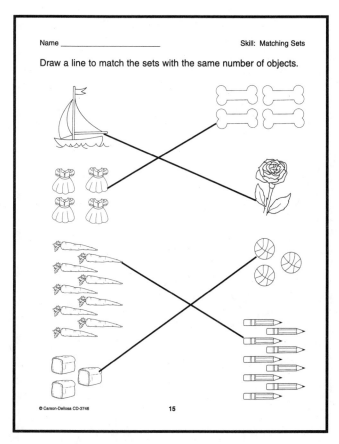

15

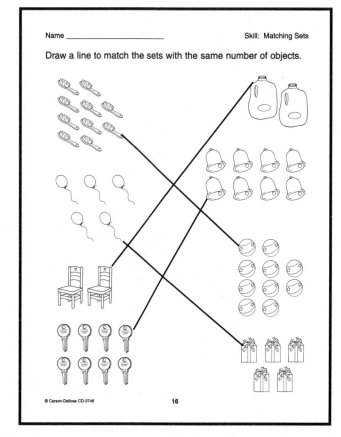

16

Answer Key

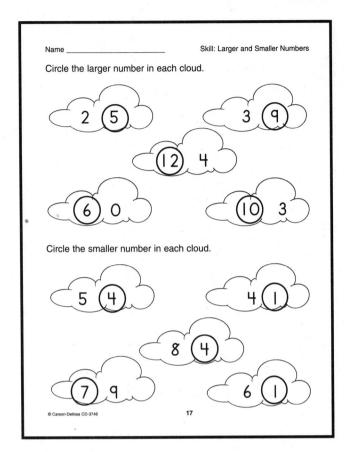

Name _____   Skill: Larger and Smaller Numbers

Circle the larger number in each cloud.

2 (5)   3 (9)

(12) 4

(6) 0   (10) 3

Circle the smaller number in each cloud.

5 (4)   4 (1)

8 (4)

(7) 9   6 (1)

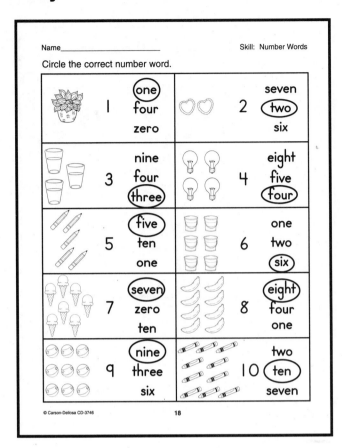

Name _____   Skill: Number Words

Circle the correct number word.

🌵	1	(one) four zero	💕	2 seven (two) six
🥛🥛	3	nine four (three)	💡💡💡💡	4 eight five (four)
✏️✏️✏️	5	(five) ten one	🥤🥤🥤🥤🥤🥤	6 one two (six)
🍦🍦🍦🍦🍦🍦🍦	7	(seven) zero ten	🍌🍌🍌🍌🍌🍌🍌🍌	8 (eight) four one
⚾⚾⚾⚾⚾⚾⚾⚾⚾	9	(nine) three six	✏️✏️✏️✏️✏️✏️✏️✏️✏️✏️	10 two (ten) seven

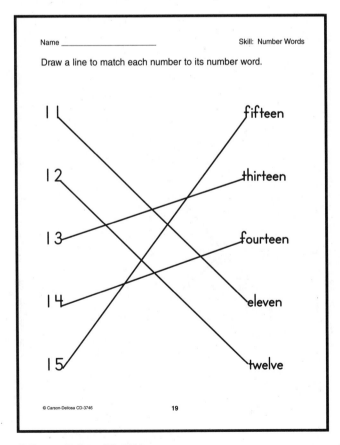

Name _____   Skill: Number Words

Draw a line to match each number to its number word.

11   fifteen

12   thirteen

13   fourteen

14   eleven

15   twelve

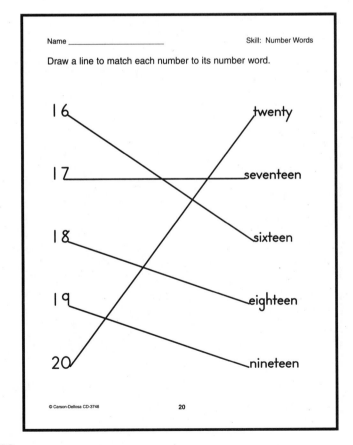

Name _____   Skill: Number Words

Draw a line to match each number to its number word.

16   twenty

17   seventeen

18   sixteen

19   eighteen

20   nineteen

Answer Key

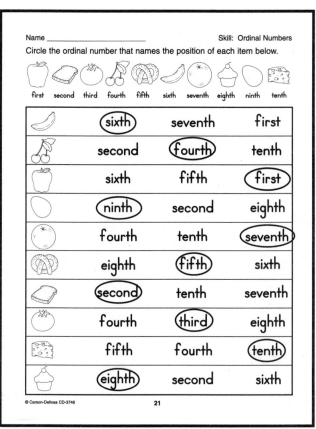

Name _____ Skill: Ordinal Numbers

Circle the ordinal number that names the position of each item below.

first second third fourth fifth sixth seventh eighth ninth tenth

banana	(sixth)	seventh	first
cherries	second	(fourth)	tenth
apple	sixth	fifth	(first)
	(ninth)	second	eighth
orange	fourth	tenth	(seventh)
pretzel	eighth	(fifth)	sixth
bread	(second)	tenth	seventh
tomato	fourth	(third)	eighth
cheese	fifth	fourth	(tenth)
cupcake	(eighth)	second	sixth

© Carson-Dellosa CD-3746   21

Name _____ Skill: Even Numbers

Even numbers can be divided into 2 equal groups. Numbers that end in 0, 2, 4, 6, or 8 are even numbers. Circle the even numbers in each row.

(2)	3	(4)	(6)	(10)
1	(2)	(8)	(12)	(14)
11	(12)	13	19	21
(16)	17	19	(20)	(22)
(18)	23	25	(26)	(28)
(24)	(26)	27	29	(30)

In each blank, write the even number that would come next.

2, 4, 6, __8__, 10, 12, __14__, 16, __18__

© Carson-Dellosa CD-3746   22

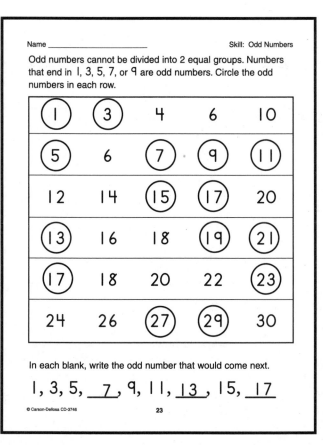

Name _____ Skill: Odd Numbers

Odd numbers cannot be divided into 2 equal groups. Numbers that end in 1, 3, 5, 7, or 9 are odd numbers. Circle the odd numbers in each row.

(1)	(3)	4	6	10
(5)	6	(7)	(9)	(11)
12	14	(15)	(17)	20
(13)	16	18	(19)	(21)
(17)	18	20	22	(23)
24	26	(27)	(29)	30

In each blank, write the odd number that would come next.

1, 3, 5, __7__, 9, 11, __13__, 15, __17__

© Carson-Dellosa CD-3746   23

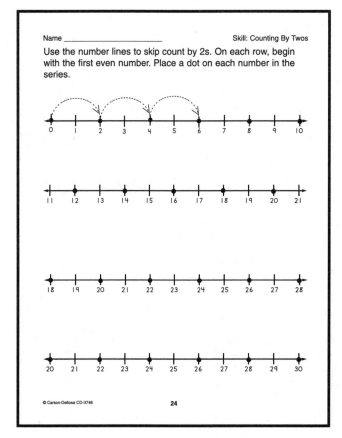

Name _____ Skill: Counting By Twos

Use the number lines to skip count by 2s. On each row, begin with the first even number. Place a dot on each number in the series.

© Carson-Dellosa CD-3746   24

© Carson-Dellosa CD-3746   104

Answer Key

Name _____

Fill in the blank squares. Skip count by 2s.

1	2	3	4	5
6	7	8	9	10
11	12	13	14	15
16	17	18	19	20

Write the next five even numbers to continue the pattern.

__22__ __24__ __26__ __28__ __30__

25

Name _____

Complete the pattern. Skip count by 2s.

__2__ __4__ __6__ __8__ __10__

__12__ __14__ __16__ __18__ __20__

__22__ __24__ __26__ __28__ __30__

26

Name _____

Count by 2s to complete the grids below.

2	4	6	8	10
12	14	16	18	20
22	24	26	28	30

2	4	6	8	10
12	14	16	18	20
22	24	26	28	30

27

Name _____

Use the number lines to count by 5s. Write the correct number in each box.

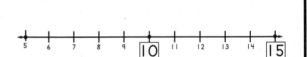

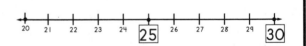

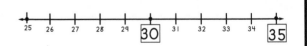

28

Answer Key

(Worksheet 29)

Skill: Counting by Fives

Fill in the missing numbers. Skip count by 5s.

1	2	3	4	5	6	7	8	9	10
11	12	13	14	15	16	17	18	19	20
21	22	23	24	25	26	27	28	29	30
31	32	33	34	35	36	37	38	39	40
41	42	43	44	45	46	47	48	49	50
51	52	53	54	55	56	57	58	59	60
61	62	63	64	65	66	67	68	69	70
71	72	73	74	75	76	77	78	79	80
81	82	83	84	85	86	87	88	89	90
91	92	93	94	95	96	97	98	99	100

29

(Worksheet 30)

Skill: Counting by Fives

Complete the pattern. Skip count by 5s.

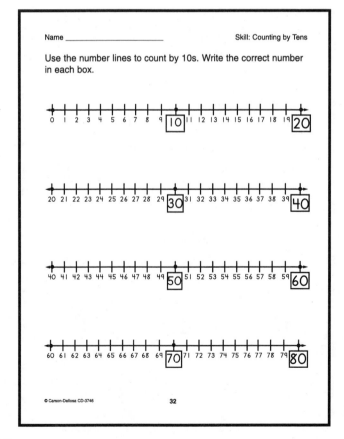

5   10   15   20

25   30   35   40

45   50   55   60

30

(Worksheet 31)

Skill: Counting by Fives

Count by 5s. Fill in the blank squares.

5	10	15	20
25	30	35	40
45	50	55	60
65	70	75	80
85	90	95	100

31

(Worksheet 32)

Skill: Counting by Tens

Use the number lines to count by 10s. Write the correct number in each box.

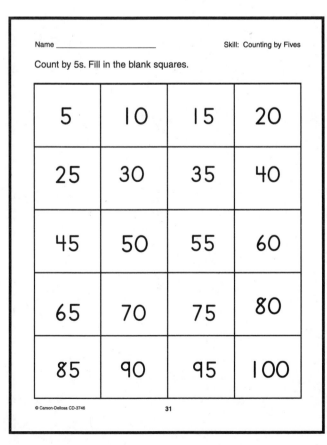

32

Answer Key

Fill in the missing numbers. Skip count by 10s.

1	2	3	4	5	6	7	8	9	10
11	12	13	14	15	16	17	18	19	20
21	22	23	24	25	26	27	28	29	30
31	32	33	34	35	36	37	38	39	40
41	42	43	44	45	46	47	48	49	50
51	52	53	54	55	56	57	58	59	60
61	62	63	64	65	66	67	68	69	70
71	72	73	74	75	76	77	78	79	80
81	82	83	84	85	86	87	88	89	90
91	92	93	94	95	96	97	98	99	100

   33

Complete the series. Skip count by 10s.

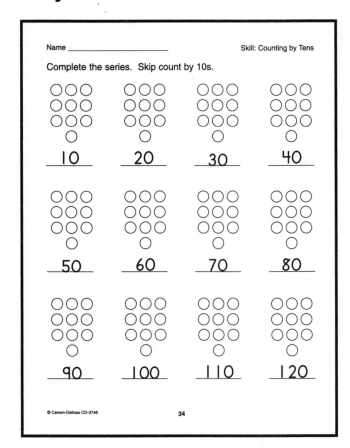

10   20   30   40

50   60   70   80

90   100   110   120

   34

Count by 10s. Fill in the blank squares.

10	20	30	40	50
60	70	80	90	100

10	20	30	40	50
60	70	80	90	100

   35

Add.

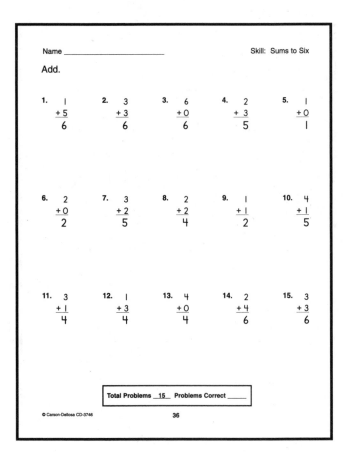

1. 1 + 5 = 6
2. 3 + 3 = 6
3. 6 + 0 = 6
4. 2 + 3 = 5
5. 1 + 0 = 1

6. 2 + 0 = 2
7. 3 + 2 = 5
8. 2 + 2 = 4
9. 1 + 1 = 2
10. 4 + 1 = 5

11. 3 + 1 = 4
12. 1 + 3 = 4
13. 4 + 0 = 4
14. 2 + 4 = 6
15. 3 + 3 = 6

Total Problems __15__   Problems Correct _____

   36

Answer Key

Name _____   Skill: Sums to Six

Add.

1. $2 + 3 = 5$

2. $1 + 2 = 3$

3. $4 + 2 = 6$

4. $1 + 5 = 6$

5. $4 + 0 = 4$

6. $5 + 1 = 6$

7. $4 + 2 = 6$

8. $2 + 2 = 4$

9. $4 + 1 = 5$

10. $0 + 4 = 4$

11. $3 + 2 = 5$

12. $3 + 3 = 6$

Total Problems __12__ Problems Correct _____

37

Name _____   Skill: Sums to Eight

Add.

1. $\begin{array}{r} 1 \\ + 4 \\ \hline 5 \end{array}$	2. $\begin{array}{r} 4 \\ + 3 \\ \hline 7 \end{array}$	3. $\begin{array}{r} 6 \\ + 2 \\ \hline 8 \end{array}$	4. $\begin{array}{r} 5 \\ + 3 \\ \hline 8 \end{array}$	5. $\begin{array}{r} 1 \\ + 7 \\ \hline 8 \end{array}$
6. $\begin{array}{r} 3 \\ + 4 \\ \hline 7 \end{array}$	7. $\begin{array}{r} 3 \\ + 5 \\ \hline 8 \end{array}$	8. $\begin{array}{r} 2 \\ + 0 \\ \hline 2 \end{array}$	9. $\begin{array}{r} 1 \\ + 3 \\ \hline 4 \end{array}$	10. $\begin{array}{r} 4 \\ + 4 \\ \hline 8 \end{array}$
11. $\begin{array}{r} 6 \\ + 1 \\ \hline 7 \end{array}$	12. $\begin{array}{r} 1 \\ + 5 \\ \hline 6 \end{array}$	13. $\begin{array}{r} 2 \\ + 0 \\ \hline 2 \end{array}$	14. $\begin{array}{r} 2 \\ + 6 \\ \hline 8 \end{array}$	15. $\begin{array}{r} 2 \\ + 4 \\ \hline 6 \end{array}$

Total Problems __15__ Problems Correct _____

38

Name _____   Skill: Sums to Eight

Add.

1. $\begin{array}{r} 2 \\ + 4 \\ \hline 6 \end{array}$	2. $\begin{array}{r} 4 \\ + 4 \\ \hline 8 \end{array}$	3. $\begin{array}{r} 6 \\ + 1 \\ \hline 7 \end{array}$	4. $\begin{array}{r} 5 \\ + 0 \\ \hline 5 \end{array}$	5. $\begin{array}{r} 1 \\ + 6 \\ \hline 7 \end{array}$
6. $\begin{array}{r} 3 \\ + 2 \\ \hline 5 \end{array}$	7. $\begin{array}{r} 3 \\ + 4 \\ \hline 7 \end{array}$	8. $\begin{array}{r} 2 \\ + 6 \\ \hline 8 \end{array}$	9. $\begin{array}{r} 4 \\ + 3 \\ \hline 7 \end{array}$	10. $\begin{array}{r} 4 \\ + 4 \\ \hline 8 \end{array}$
11. $\begin{array}{r} 6 \\ + 2 \\ \hline 8 \end{array}$	12. $\begin{array}{r} 1 \\ + 3 \\ \hline 4 \end{array}$	13. $\begin{array}{r} 2 \\ + 3 \\ \hline 5 \end{array}$	14. $\begin{array}{r} 2 \\ + 1 \\ \hline 3 \end{array}$	15. $\begin{array}{r} 3 \\ + 4 \\ \hline 7 \end{array}$

Total Problems __15__ Problems Correct _____

39

Name _____   Skill: Sums to Ten

Add.

1. $\begin{array}{r} 7 \\ + 2 \\ \hline 9 \end{array}$	2. $\begin{array}{r} 8 \\ + 0 \\ \hline 8 \end{array}$	3. $\begin{array}{r} 0 \\ + 10 \\ \hline 10 \end{array}$	4. $\begin{array}{r} 9 \\ + 0 \\ \hline 9 \end{array}$	5. $\begin{array}{r} 2 \\ + 6 \\ \hline 8 \end{array}$
6. $\begin{array}{r} 3 \\ + 7 \\ \hline 10 \end{array}$	7. $\begin{array}{r} 1 \\ + 9 \\ \hline 10 \end{array}$	8. $\begin{array}{r} 0 \\ + 7 \\ \hline 7 \end{array}$	9. $\begin{array}{r} 1 \\ + 8 \\ \hline 9 \end{array}$	10. $\begin{array}{r} 7 \\ + 3 \\ \hline 10 \end{array}$
11. $\begin{array}{r} 3 \\ + 4 \\ \hline 7 \end{array}$	12. $\begin{array}{r} 1 \\ + 7 \\ \hline 8 \end{array}$	13. $\begin{array}{r} 7 \\ + 0 \\ \hline 7 \end{array}$	14. $\begin{array}{r} 5 \\ + 4 \\ \hline 9 \end{array}$	15. $\begin{array}{r} 6 \\ + 3 \\ \hline 9 \end{array}$

Total Problems __15__ Problems Correct _____

40

Answer Key

Name _____ Skill: Sums to Ten

Add.

1. $5 + 1 = 6$ 2. $8 + 1 = 9$ 3. $9 + 0 = 9$

4. $4 + 1 = 5$ 5. $4 + 2 = 6$ 6. $5 + 3 = 8$

7. $3 + 2 = 5$ 8. $3 + 7 = 10$ 9. $6 + 2 = 8$

10. $6 + 3 = 9$ 11. $5 + 4 = 9$ 12. $3 + 4 = 7$

13. $4 + 6 = 10$ 14. $7 + 3 = 10$ 15. $2 + 7 = 9$

Total Problems __15__ Problems Correct _____

41

Name _____ Skill: Sums to Eleven

Add.

1. $\begin{array}{r}5\\+4\\\hline9\end{array}$	2. $\begin{array}{r}7\\+3\\\hline10\end{array}$	3. $\begin{array}{r}6\\+4\\\hline10\end{array}$	4. $\begin{array}{r}5\\+2\\\hline7\end{array}$	5. $\begin{array}{r}4\\+7\\\hline11\end{array}$
6. $\begin{array}{r}3\\+5\\\hline8\end{array}$	7. $\begin{array}{r}6\\+5\\\hline11\end{array}$	8. $\begin{array}{r}2\\+9\\\hline11\end{array}$	9. $\begin{array}{r}2\\+6\\\hline8\end{array}$	10. $\begin{array}{r}8\\+3\\\hline11\end{array}$
11. $\begin{array}{r}4\\+4\\\hline8\end{array}$	12. $\begin{array}{r}3\\+6\\\hline9\end{array}$	13. $\begin{array}{r}10\\+1\\\hline11\end{array}$	14. $\begin{array}{r}11\\+0\\\hline11\end{array}$	15. $\begin{array}{r}5\\+4\\\hline9\end{array}$

Total Problems __15__ Problems Correct _____

42

Name _____ Skill: Sums to Eleven

Add.

1. $\begin{array}{r}9\\+2\\\hline11\end{array}$	2. $\begin{array}{r}11\\+0\\\hline11\end{array}$	3. $\begin{array}{r}10\\+1\\\hline11\end{array}$	4. $\begin{array}{r}9\\+0\\\hline9\end{array}$	5. $\begin{array}{r}5\\+6\\\hline11\end{array}$
6. $\begin{array}{r}3\\+6\\\hline9\end{array}$	7. $\begin{array}{r}1\\+9\\\hline10\end{array}$	8. $\begin{array}{r}4\\+7\\\hline11\end{array}$	9. $\begin{array}{r}2\\+8\\\hline10\end{array}$	10. $\begin{array}{r}7\\+4\\\hline11\end{array}$
11. $\begin{array}{r}3\\+5\\\hline8\end{array}$	12. $\begin{array}{r}3\\+7\\\hline10\end{array}$	13. $\begin{array}{r}0\\+8\\\hline8\end{array}$	14. $\begin{array}{r}6\\+4\\\hline10\end{array}$	15. $\begin{array}{r}6\\+5\\\hline11\end{array}$

Total Problems __15__ Problems Correct _____

43

Name _____ Skill: Sums to Twelve

Add.

1. $\begin{array}{r}7\\+5\\\hline12\end{array}$	2. $\begin{array}{r}8\\+3\\\hline11\end{array}$	3. $\begin{array}{r}10\\+2\\\hline12\end{array}$	4. $\begin{array}{r}9\\+2\\\hline11\end{array}$	5. $\begin{array}{r}6\\+6\\\hline12\end{array}$
6. $\begin{array}{r}4\\+7\\\hline11\end{array}$	7. $\begin{array}{r}10\\+1\\\hline11\end{array}$	8. $\begin{array}{r}3\\+7\\\hline10\end{array}$	9. $\begin{array}{r}1\\+9\\\hline10\end{array}$	10. $\begin{array}{r}7\\+3\\\hline10\end{array}$
11. $\begin{array}{r}3\\+6\\\hline9\end{array}$	12. $\begin{array}{r}5\\+7\\\hline12\end{array}$	13. $\begin{array}{r}7\\+5\\\hline12\end{array}$	14. $\begin{array}{r}5\\+3\\\hline8\end{array}$	15. $\begin{array}{r}7\\+3\\\hline10\end{array}$

Total Problems __15__ Problems Correct _____

44

Answer Key

Worksheet (page 45)

Name _____   Skill: Sums to Twelve

Add.

1. 7 + 4 = 11
2. 12 + 0 = 12
3. 10 + 2 = 12
4. 9 + 3 = 12
5. 4 + 6 = 10
6. 3 + 6 = 9
7. 1 + 8 = 9
8. 2 + 7 = 9
9. 4 + 8 = 12
10. 7 + 5 = 12
11. 3 + 5 = 8
12. 3 + 7 = 10
13. 7 + 1 = 8
14. 5 + 6 = 11
15. 6 + 4 = 10

Total Problems 15   Problems Correct _____

45

Worksheet (page 46)

Name _____   Skill: Sums to Thirteen

Add.

1. 7 + 6 = 13
2. 8 + 5 = 13
3. 10 + 2 = 12
4. 9 + 3 = 12
5. 5 + 6 = 11
6. 4 + 7 = 11
7. 2 + 9 = 11
8. 5 + 7 = 12
9. 3 + 8 = 11
10. 7 + 4 = 11
11. 8 + 3 = 11
12. 3 + 6 = 9
13. 7 + 6 = 13
14. 8 + 5 = 13
15. 6 + 6 = 12

Total Problems 15   Problems Correct _____

46

Worksheet (page 47)

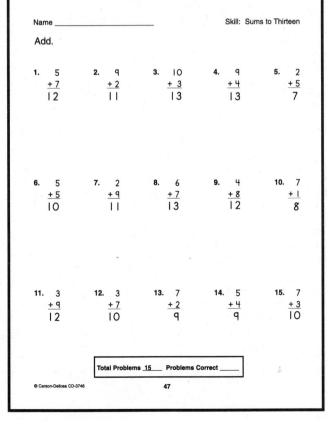

Name _____   Skill: Sums to Thirteen

Add.

1. 5 + 7 = 12
2. 9 + 2 = 11
3. 10 + 3 = 13
4. 9 + 4 = 13
5. 2 + 5 = 7
6. 5 + 5 = 10
7. 2 + 9 = 11
8. 6 + 7 = 13
9. 4 + 8 = 12
10. 7 + 1 = 8
11. 3 + 9 = 12
12. 3 + 7 = 10
13. 7 + 2 = 9
14. 5 + 4 = 9
15. 7 + 3 = 10

Total Problems 15   Problems Correct _____

47

Worksheet (page 48)

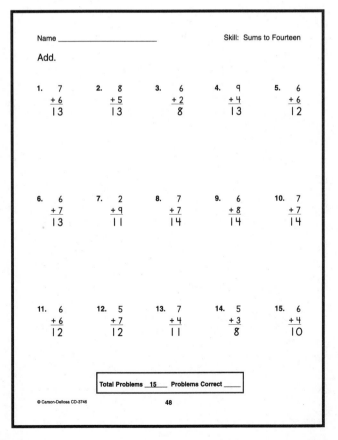

Name _____   Skill: Sums to Fourteen

Add.

1. 7 + 6 = 13
2. 8 + 5 = 13
3. 6 + 2 = 8
4. 9 + 4 = 13
5. 6 + 6 = 12
6. 6 + 7 = 13
7. 2 + 9 = 11
8. 7 + 7 = 14
9. 6 + 8 = 14
10. 7 + 7 = 14
11. 6 + 6 = 12
12. 5 + 7 = 12
13. 7 + 4 = 11
14. 5 + 3 = 8
15. 6 + 4 = 10

Total Problems 15   Problems Correct _____

48

Answer Key

Add.

1. 7 +5 = 12	2. 8 +3 = 11	3. 10 +4 = 14	4. 9 +3 = 12	5. 6 +6 = 12
6. 5 +7 = 12	7. 5 +9 = 14	8. 7 +7 = 14	9. 3 +8 = 11	10. 7 +7 = 14
11. 3 +9 = 12	12. 3 +7 = 10	13. 6 +8 = 14	14. 5 +7 = 12	15. 6 +5 = 11

Total Problems __15__   Problems Correct _____

49

Add.

1. 7 +8 = 15	2. 8 +7 = 15	3. 10 +5 = 15	4. 9 +6 = 15	5. 3 +6 = 9
6. 6 +7 = 13	7. 4 +9 = 13	8. 5 +7 = 12	9. 3 +8 = 11	10. 7 +5 = 12
11. 4 +9 = 13	12. 5 +7 = 12	13. 7 +6 = 13	14. 5 +6 = 11	15. 6 +7 = 13

Total Problems __15__   Problems Correct _____

50

Add.

1. 8 +7 = 15	2. 6 +9 = 15	3. 10 +1 = 11	4. 9 +3 = 12	5. 1 +6 = 7
6. 5 +7 = 12	7. 2 +9 = 11	8. 7 +7 = 14	9. 2 +8 = 10	10. 7 +4 = 11
11. 6 +4 = 10	12. 3 +7 = 10	13. 7 +2 = 9	14. 5 +6 = 11	15. 6 +5 = 11

Total Problems __15__   Problems Correct _____

51

Add.

1. 9 +4 = 13	2. 8 +7 = 15	3. 10 +6 = 16	4. 10 +2 = 12	5. 7 +9 = 16
6. 10 +5 = 15	7. 6 +9 = 15	8. 11 +4 = 15	9. 8 +8 = 16	10. 9 +6 = 15
11. 8 +5 = 13	12. 7 +7 = 14	13. 7 +6 = 13	14. 5 +9 = 14	15. 6 +4 = 10

Total Problems __15__   Problems Correct _____

52

Answer Key

Name _____   Skill: Sums to Sixteen

Add.

1. 9 + 5 = 14
2. 12 + 4 = 16
3. 11 + 4 = 15
4. 10 + 6 = 16
5. 9 + 3 = 12

6. 8 + 7 = 15
7. 5 + 5 = 10
8. 13 + 2 = 15
9. 6 + 7 = 13
10. 2 + 8 = 10

11. 7 + 9 = 16
12. 6 + 8 = 14
13. 4 + 2 = 6
14. 5 + 6 = 11
15. 9 + 4 = 13

Total Problems __15__ Problems Correct _____

53

Name _____   Skill: Sums to Seventeen

Add.

1. 5 + 7 = 12
2. 15 + 1 = 16
3. 14 + 3 = 17
4. 11 + 4 = 15
5. 9 + 8 = 17

6. 4 + 7 = 11
7. 5 + 8 = 13
8. 8 + 9 = 17
9. 13 + 3 = 16
10. 14 + 3 = 17

11. 9 + 4 = 13
12. 6 + 4 = 10
13. 3 + 8 = 11
14. 5 + 9 = 14
15. 10 + 7 = 17

Total Problems __15__ Problems Correct _____

54

Name _____   Skill: Sums to Seventeen

Add.

1. 10 + 7 = 17
2. 13 + 4 = 17
3. 11 + 4 = 15
4. 12 + 5 = 17
5. 7 + 9 = 16

6. 10 + 3 = 13
7. 15 + 1 = 16
8. 9 + 4 = 13
9. 7 + 6 = 13
10. 10 + 5 = 15

11. 7 + 7 = 14
12. 8 + 7 = 15
13. 11 + 6 = 17
14. 6 + 3 = 9
15. 9 + 5 = 14

Total Problems __15__ Problems Correct _____

55

Name _____   Skill: Sums to Eighteen

Add.

1. 8 + 7 = 15
2. 6 + 9 = 15
3. 10 + 8 = 18
4. 10 + 2 = 12
5. 12 + 5 = 17

6. 13 + 4 = 17
7. 11 + 5 = 16
8. 9 + 5 = 14
9. 10 + 4 = 14
10. 9 + 2 = 11

11. 4 + 9 = 13
12. 12 + 1 = 13
13. 4 + 7 = 11
14. 14 + 4 = 18
15. 15 + 2 = 17

Total Problems __15__ Problems Correct _____

56

112

Answer Key

Name _____   Skill: Sums to Eighteen

Add.

1.	2.	3.	4.	5.
15 +3 = 18	12 +4 = 16	11 +2 = 13	8 +2 = 10	7 +6 = 13

6.	7.	8.	9.	10.
10 +5 = 15	8 +9 = 17	11 +7 = 18	13 +5 = 18	9 +7 = 16

11.	12.	13.	14.	15.
10 +8 = 18	9 +3 = 12	12 +5 = 17	9 +9 = 18	8 +5 = 13

Total Problems __15__   Problems Correct _____

57

Name _____   Skill: Subtracting from Six or Less

Subtract.

1.	2.	3.	4.	5.
5 -5 = 0	3 -3 = 0	6 -0 = 6	6 -3 = 3	1 -0 = 1

6.	7.	8.	9.	10.
2 -0 = 2	3 -2 = 1	2 -2 = 0	1 -1 = 0	4 -1 = 3

11.	12.	13.	14.	15.
3 -1 = 2	5 -3 = 2	4 -0 = 4	5 -4 = 1	3 -3 = 0

Total Problems __15__   Problems Correct _____

58

Name _____   Skill: Subtracting from Six or Less

Subtract.

1.	2.	3.	4.	5.
6 -3 = 3	4 -0 = 4	3 -3 = 0	5 -2 = 3	6 -2 = 4

6.	7.	8.	9.	10.
2 -2 = 0	4 -2 = 2	3 -2 = 1	6 -4 = 2	4 -3 = 1

11.	12.	13.	14.	15.
1 -1 = 0	3 -0 = 3	4 -1 = 3	3 -1 = 2	5 -1 = 4

Total Problems __15__   Problems Correct _____

59

Name _____   Skill: Subtracting from Ten or Less

Subtract.

1.	2.	3.	4.	5.
6 -3 = 3	10 -6 = 4	7 -5 = 2	10 -8 = 2	8 -4 = 4

6.	7.	8.	9.	10.
9 -4 = 5	7 -3 = 4	6 -4 = 2	9 -5 = 4	10 -3 = 7

11.	12.	13.	14.	15.
8 -6 = 2	9 -3 = 6	10 -1 = 9	7 -6 = 1	8 -2 = 6

Total Problems __15__   Problems Correct _____

60

Answer Key

Name _____   Skill: Subtracting from Ten or Less

Subtract.

1.	9 − 2 7	2.	7 − 5 2	3.	10 − 3 7	4.	10 − 5 5	5.	6 − 4 2
6.	8 − 6 2	7.	7 − 2 5	8.	9 − 7 2	9.	3 − 2 1	10.	8 − 2 6
11.	10 − 4 6	12.	9 − 8 1	13.	9 − 5 4	14.	8 − 3 5	15.	7 − 3 4

Total Problems __15__ Problems Correct _____

61

Name _____   Skill: Subtracting from Eleven or Less

Subtract.

1.	9 − 3 6	2.	10 − 6 4	3.	7 − 5 2	4.	9 − 8 1	5.	8 − 4 4
6.	9 − 4 5	7.	11 − 2 9	8.	6 − 4 2	9.	9 − 5 4	10.	11 − 3 8
11.	8 − 8 0	12.	7 − 3 4	13.	11 − 1 10	14.	11 − 6 5	15.	11 − 2 9

Total Problems __15__ Problems Correct _____

62

Name _____   Skill: Subtracting from Eleven or Less

Subtract.

1.	10 − 6 4	2.	11 − 3 8	3.	6 − 5 1	4.	11 − 8 3	5.	10 − 4 6
6.	10 − 8 2	7.	6 − 3 3	8.	10 − 4 6	9.	8 − 3 5	10.	11 − 5 6
11.	9 − 6 3	12.	11 − 6 5	13.	8 − 4 4	14.	6 − 2 4	15.	9 − 1 8

Total Problems __15__ Problems Correct _____

63

Name _____   Skill: Subtracting from Twelve or Less

Subtract.

1.	12 − 3 9	2.	11 − 6 5	3.	10 − 5 5	4.	12 − 8 4	5.	12 − 4 8
6.	9 − 2 7	7.	9 − 5 4	8.	11 − 4 7	9.	10 − 4 6	10.	12 − 5 7
11.	11 − 6 5	12.	9 − 4 5	13.	11 − 1 10	14.	9 − 6 3	15.	8 − 3 5

Total Problems __15__ Problems Correct _____

64

Answer Key

Name _____ Skill: Subtracting from Twelve or Less

Subtract.

1. $\begin{array}{r} 11 \\ -\ 2 \\ \hline 9 \end{array}$	2. $\begin{array}{r} 12 \\ -\ 5 \\ \hline 7 \end{array}$	3. $\begin{array}{r} 9 \\ -\ 2 \\ \hline 7 \end{array}$	4. $\begin{array}{r} 8 \\ -\ 6 \\ \hline 2 \end{array}$	5. $\begin{array}{r} 9 \\ -\ 3 \\ \hline 6 \end{array}$
6. $\begin{array}{r} 9 \\ -\ 8 \\ \hline 1 \end{array}$	7. $\begin{array}{r} 12 \\ -\ 8 \\ \hline 4 \end{array}$	8. $\begin{array}{r} 11 \\ -\ 7 \\ \hline 4 \end{array}$	9. $\begin{array}{r} 12 \\ -\ 2 \\ \hline 10 \end{array}$	10. $\begin{array}{r} 7 \\ -\ 2 \\ \hline 5 \end{array}$
11. $\begin{array}{r} 10 \\ -\ 5 \\ \hline 5 \end{array}$	12. $\begin{array}{r} 9 \\ -\ 6 \\ \hline 3 \end{array}$	13. $\begin{array}{r} 12 \\ -\ 3 \\ \hline 9 \end{array}$	14. $\begin{array}{r} 7 \\ -\ 4 \\ \hline 3 \end{array}$	15. $\begin{array}{r} 9 \\ -\ 5 \\ \hline 4 \end{array}$

Total Problems 15   Problems Correct _____

© Carson-Dellosa CD-3746   65

Name _____ Skill: Subtracting from Thirteen or Less

Subtract.

1. $\begin{array}{r} 13 \\ -\ 3 \\ \hline 10 \end{array}$	2. $\begin{array}{r} 13 \\ -\ 6 \\ \hline 7 \end{array}$	3. $\begin{array}{r} 9 \\ -\ 5 \\ \hline 4 \end{array}$	4. $\begin{array}{r} 10 \\ -\ 5 \\ \hline 5 \end{array}$	5. $\begin{array}{r} 8 \\ -\ 1 \\ \hline 7 \end{array}$
6. $\begin{array}{r} 12 \\ -\ 4 \\ \hline 8 \end{array}$	7. $\begin{array}{r} 10 \\ -\ 3 \\ \hline 7 \end{array}$	8. $\begin{array}{r} 9 \\ -\ 4 \\ \hline 5 \end{array}$	9. $\begin{array}{r} 8 \\ -\ 5 \\ \hline 3 \end{array}$	10. $\begin{array}{r} 11 \\ -\ 3 \\ \hline 8 \end{array}$
11. $\begin{array}{r} 12 \\ -\ 6 \\ \hline 6 \end{array}$	12. $\begin{array}{r} 8 \\ -\ 3 \\ \hline 5 \end{array}$	13. $\begin{array}{r} 13 \\ -\ 5 \\ \hline 8 \end{array}$	14. $\begin{array}{r} 10 \\ -\ 6 \\ \hline 4 \end{array}$	15. $\begin{array}{r} 9 \\ -\ 3 \\ \hline 6 \end{array}$

Total Problems 15   Problems Correct _____

© Carson-Dellosa CD-3746   66

Name _____ Skill: Subtracting from Thirteen or Less

Subtract.

1. $\begin{array}{r} 13 \\ -\ 5 \\ \hline 8 \end{array}$	2. $\begin{array}{r} 9 \\ -\ 3 \\ \hline 6 \end{array}$	3. $\begin{array}{r} 10 \\ -\ 3 \\ \hline 7 \end{array}$	4. $\begin{array}{r} 11 \\ -\ 8 \\ \hline 3 \end{array}$	5. $\begin{array}{r} 9 \\ -\ 4 \\ \hline 5 \end{array}$
6. $\begin{array}{r} 9 \\ -\ 6 \\ \hline 3 \end{array}$	7. $\begin{array}{r} 9 \\ -\ 3 \\ \hline 6 \end{array}$	8. $\begin{array}{r} 13 \\ -\ 7 \\ \hline 6 \end{array}$	9. $\begin{array}{r} 7 \\ -\ 3 \\ \hline 4 \end{array}$	10. $\begin{array}{r} 3 \\ -\ 2 \\ \hline 1 \end{array}$
11. $\begin{array}{r} 10 \\ -\ 4 \\ \hline 6 \end{array}$	12. $\begin{array}{r} 13 \\ -\ 6 \\ \hline 7 \end{array}$	13. $\begin{array}{r} 9 \\ -\ 4 \\ \hline 5 \end{array}$	14. $\begin{array}{r} 8 \\ -\ 2 \\ \hline 6 \end{array}$	15. $\begin{array}{r} 9 \\ -\ 2 \\ \hline 7 \end{array}$

Total Problems 15   Problems Correct _____

© Carson-Dellosa CD-3746   67

Name _____ Skill: Subtracting from Fourteen or Less

Subtract.

1. $\begin{array}{r} 14 \\ -\ 3 \\ \hline 11 \end{array}$	2. $\begin{array}{r} 14 \\ -\ 6 \\ \hline 8 \end{array}$	3. $\begin{array}{r} 10 \\ -\ 2 \\ \hline 8 \end{array}$	4. $\begin{array}{r} 10 \\ -\ 5 \\ \hline 5 \end{array}$	5. $\begin{array}{r} 11 \\ -\ 6 \\ \hline 5 \end{array}$
6. $\begin{array}{r} 12 \\ -\ 5 \\ \hline 7 \end{array}$	7. $\begin{array}{r} 13 \\ -\ 1 \\ \hline 12 \end{array}$	8. $\begin{array}{r} 14 \\ -\ 7 \\ \hline 7 \end{array}$	9. $\begin{array}{r} 12 \\ -\ 8 \\ \hline 4 \end{array}$	10. $\begin{array}{r} 11 \\ -\ 9 \\ \hline 2 \end{array}$
11. $\begin{array}{r} 12 \\ -\ 3 \\ \hline 9 \end{array}$	12. $\begin{array}{r} 14 \\ -\ 5 \\ \hline 9 \end{array}$	13. $\begin{array}{r} 10 \\ -\ 8 \\ \hline 2 \end{array}$	14. $\begin{array}{r} 10 \\ -\ 7 \\ \hline 3 \end{array}$	15. $\begin{array}{r} 9 \\ -\ 2 \\ \hline 7 \end{array}$

Total Problems 15   Problems Correct _____

© Carson-Dellosa CD-3746   68

© Carson-Dellosa CD-3746   **115**

Answer Key

Name _____   Skill: Subtracting from Fourteen or Less

Subtract.

1. 13 − 5 **8**	**2.** 11 − 8 **3**	**3.** 9 − 3 **6**	**4.** 12 − 4 **8**	**5.** 14 − 7 **7**
6. 13 − 8 **5**	**7.** 10 − 6 **4**	**8.** 11 − 5 **6**	**9.** 12 − 9 **3**	**10.** 10 − 8 **2**
11. 14 − 2 **12**	**12.** 10 − 4 **6**	**13.** 9 − 5 **4**	**14.** 11 − 7 **4**	**15.** 14 − 6 **8**

Total Problems _15_   Problems Correct _____

69

Name _____   Skill: Subtracting from Fifteen or Less

Subtract.

1. 13 − 3 **10**	**2.** 14 − 6 **8**	**3.** 15 − 5 **10**	**4.** 11 − 5 **6**	**5.** 10 − 1 **9**
6. 12 − 4 **8**	**7.** 10 − 3 **7**	**8.** 14 − 4 **10**	**9.** 15 − 2 **13**	**10.** 11 − 3 **8**
11. 12 − 6 **6**	**12.** 15 − 8 **7**	**13.** 10 − 5 **5**	**14.** 11 − 6 **5**	**15.** 15 − 3 **12**

Total Problems _15_   Problems Correct _____

70

Name _____   Skill: Subtracting from Fifteen or Less

Subtract.

1. 13 − 6 **7**	**2.** 15 − 3 **12**	**3.** 12 − 8 **4**	**4.** 10 − 8 **2**	**5.** 11 − 5 **6**
6. 15 − 6 **9**	**7.** 10 − 3 **7**	**8.** 13 − 5 **8**	**9.** 12 − 3 **9**	**10.** 15 − 2 **13**
11. 13 − 4 **9**	**12.** 14 − 6 **8**	**13.** 15 − 9 **6**	**14.** 11 − 2 **9**	**15.** 10 − 2 **8**

Total Problems _15_   Problems Correct _____

71

Name _____   Skill: Subtracting from Sixteen or Less

Subtract.

1. 13 − 2 **11**	**2.** 12 − 8 **4**	**3.** 10 − 7 **3**	**4.** 11 − 9 **2**	**5.** 16 − 5 **11**
6. 13 − 8 **5**	**7.** 10 − 6 **4**	**8.** 12 − 2 **10**	**9.** 10 − 8 **2**	**10.** 16 − 4 **12**
11. 15 − 6 **9**	**12.** 16 − 9 **7**	**13.** 11 − 5 **6**	**14.** 12 − 3 **9**	**15.** 13 − 3 **10**

Total Problems _15_   Problems Correct _____

72

Answer Key

Name _____   Skill: Subtracting from Sixteen or Less

Subtract.

1.	2.	3.	4.	5.
16 − 5 11	13 − 3 10	15 − 3 12	12 − 8 4	14 − 4 10

6.	7.	8.	9.	10.
12 − 6 6	15 − 3 12	14 − 7 7	16 − 3 13	13 − 2 11

11.	12.	13.	14.	15.
14 − 4 10	12 − 6 6	16 − 4 12	13 − 2 11	15 − 2 13

Total Problems __15__ Problems Correct _____

73

Name _____   Skill: Subtracting from Seventeen or Less

Subtract.

1.	2.	3.	4.	5.
17 − 6 11	15 − 3 12	13 − 8 5	17 − 5 12	16 − 1 15

6.	7.	8.	9.	10.
14 − 4 10	10 − 3 7	15 − 4 11	13 − 9 4	14 − 3 11

11.	12.	13.	14.	15.
12 − 6 6	17 − 6 11	16 − 5 11	15 − 4 11	11 − 3 8

Total Problems __15__ Problems Correct _____

© Carson-Dellosa CD-3746

74

Name _____   Skill: Subtracting from Seventeen or Less

Subtract.

1.	2.	3.	4.	5.
17 − 5 12	12 − 8 4	16 − 5 11	15 − 2 13	14 − 4 10

6.	7.	8.	9.	10.
12 − 4 8	13 − 3 10	17 − 6 11	15 − 9 6	14 − 2 12

11.	12.	13.	14.	15.
17 − 5 12	15 − 4 11	13 − 7 6	17 − 7 10	11 − 8 3

Total Problems __15__ Problems Correct _____

© Carson-Dellosa CD-3746

75

Name _____   Skill: Subtracting from Eighteen or Less

Subtract.

1.	2.	3.	4.	5.
18 − 3 15	14 − 4 10	16 − 5 11	10 − 6 4	15 − 7 8

6.	7.	8.	9.	10.
12 − 7 5	14 − 8 6	18 − 9 9	11 − 3 8	16 − 9 7

11.	12.	13.	14.	15.
13 − 4 9	12 − 5 7	10 − 2 8	18 − 7 11	17 − 3 14

Total Problems __15__ Problems Correct _____

© Carson-Dellosa CD-3746

76

© Carson-Dellosa CD-3746   **117**

Answer Key

Name _____ Skill: Subtracting from Eighteen or Less

Subtract.

1.	2.	3.	4.	5.
17 − 4 = 13	9 − 5 = 4	14 − 2 = 12	18 − 2 = 16	16 − 5 = 11

6.	7.	8.	9.	10.
14 − 3 = 11	18 − 1 = 17	16 − 4 = 12	17 − 6 = 11	15 − 7 = 8

11.	12.	13.	14.	15.
17 − 8 = 9	10 − 3 = 7	12 − 2 = 10	15 − 6 = 9	18 − 2 = 16

Total Problems 15 Problems Correct _____

© Carson-Dellosa CD-3746   77

Name _____ Skill: Addition and Subtraction through Ten

Add or subtract.

1.	2.	3.	4.	5.
8 − 5 = 3	7 + 2 = 9	9 − 3 = 6	4 + 3 = 7	5 − 2 = 3

6.	7.	8.	9.	10.
8 + 2 = 10	7 + 3 = 10	10 − 6 = 4	2 − 2 = 0	9 + 1 = 10

11.	12.	13.	14.	15.
6 − 6 = 0	8 + 0 = 8	9 + 0 = 9	2 + 3 = 5	10 − 6 = 4

Total Problems 15 Problems Correct _____

© Carson-Dellosa CD-3746   78

Name _____ Skill: Addition and Subtraction through Ten

Add or subtract.

1.	2.	3.	4.	5.
9 − 3 = 6	8 + 1 = 9	5 − 2 = 3	7 + 1 = 8	8 − 3 = 5

6.	7.	8.	9.	10.
9 + 1 = 10	10 + 0 = 10	10 − 2 = 8	7 − 5 = 2	6 + 2 = 8

11.	12.	13.	14.	15.
5 − 3 = 2	9 + 1 = 10	7 + 0 = 7	2 + 2 = 4	9 − 6 = 3

Total Problems 15 Problems Correct _____

© Carson-Dellosa CD-3746   79

Name _____ Skill: Addition and Subtraction through Ten

Add or subtract.

1.	2.	3.	4.	5.
6 − 2 = 4	9 + 1 = 10	5 − 3 = 2	8 + 1 = 9	8 − 2 = 6

6.	7.	8.	9.	10.
8 + 2 = 10	9 + 0 = 9	8 − 3 = 5	9 − 6 = 3	3 + 2 = 5

11.	12.	13.	14.	15.
5 − 2 = 3	8 + 1 = 9	7 + 1 = 8	4 + 2 = 6	9 − 5 = 4

Total Problems 15 Problems Correct _____

© Carson-Dellosa CD-3746   80

Answer Key

Panel 1 (page 81)

Name _____ Skill: Single Digit Addition—without Regrouping

Add.

1. 3 + 1 = 4
2. 5 + 4 = 9
3. 2 + 7 = 9
4. 7 + 1 = 8
5. 5 + 2 = 7

6. 7 + 0 = 7
7. 3 + 6 = 9
8. 8 + 1 = 9
9. 8 + 0 = 8
10. 4 + 3 = 7

11. 6 + 1 = 7
12. 4 + 4 = 8
13. 5 + 3 = 8
14. 6 + 2 = 8
15. 5 + 3 = 8

Total Problems 15 Problems Correct _____

81

Panel 2 (page 82)

Name _____ Skill: Single Digit Addition—with Regrouping

Add.

1. 9 + 9 = 18
2. 5 + 6 = 11
3. 2 + 8 = 10
4. 7 + 6 = 13
5. 5 + 6 = 11

6. 7 + 8 = 15
7. 3 + 9 = 12
8. 8 + 5 = 13
9. 8 + 8 = 16
10. 4 + 7 = 11

11. 6 + 8 = 14
12. 4 + 7 = 11
13. 9 + 8 = 17
14. 6 + 7 = 13
15. 5 + 6 = 11

Total Problems 15 Problems Correct _____

82

Panel 3 (page 83)

Name _____ Skill: Double Digit Addition—without Regrouping

Add.

1. 11 + 8 = 19
2. 12 + 3 = 15
3. 15 + 4 = 19
4. 10 + 7 = 17
5. 14 + 4 = 18

6. 12 + 7 = 19
7. 10 + 5 = 15
8. 11 + 6 = 17
9. 10 + 2 = 12
10. 12 + 1 = 13

11. 17 + 1 = 18
12. 15 + 2 = 17
13. 13 + 5 = 18
14. 16 + 2 = 18
15. 14 + 3 = 17

Total Problems 15 Problems Correct _____

83

Panel 4 (page 84)

Name _____ Skill: Double Digit Addition—with Regrouping

Add.

1. 11 + 9 = 20
2. 15 + 6 = 21
3. 19 + 7 = 26
4. 16 + 6 = 22
5. 17 + 6 = 23

6. 14 + 8 = 22
7. 13 + 9 = 22
8. 16 + 5 = 21
9. 12 + 8 = 20
10. 15 + 7 = 22

11. 15 + 8 = 23
12. 17 + 4 = 21
13. 14 + 8 = 22
14. 13 + 7 = 20
15. 18 + 6 = 24

Total Problems 15 Problems Correct _____

84

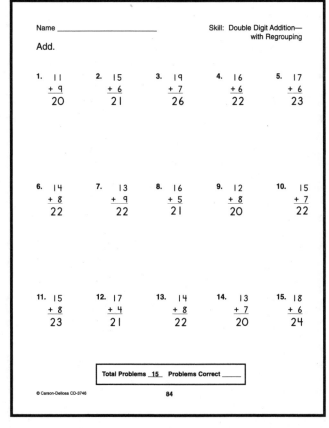

Answer Key

Write the correct time in each blank.

1:00   10:00   2:00

4:00   8:00   5:00

Write the correct time in each blank.

3:00   7:00   10:00

11:00   6:00   12:00

Write the correct time in each blank.

6:30   1:30   10:30

5:30   8:30   7:30

Write the correct time in each blank.

4:30   2:30   9:30

11:30   1:30   12:30

Answer Key

Name _____   Skill: Telling Time on the Hour

Draw hands on each clock to show the correct time.

9:00   12:00   4:00

5:00   11:00   7:00

© Carson-Dellosa CD-3746   89

Name _____   Skill: Telling Time on the Half Hour

Draw hands on each clock to show the correct time.

3:30   12:30   7:30

11:30   10:30   9:30

© Carson-Dellosa CD-3746   90

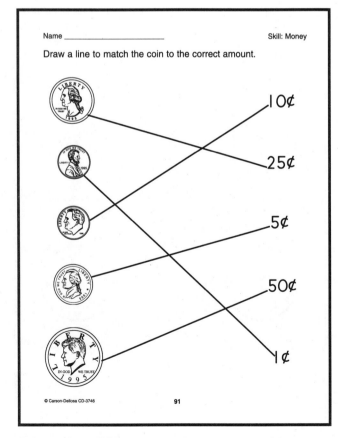

Name _____   Skill: Money

Draw a line to match the coin to the correct amount.

10¢

25¢

5¢

50¢

1¢

© Carson-Dellosa CD-3746   91

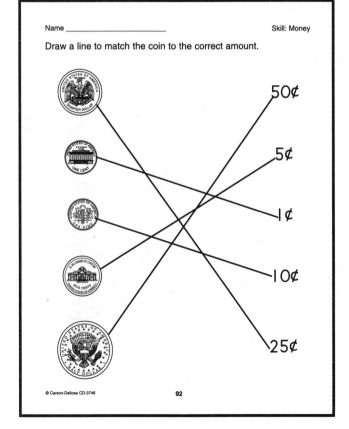

Name _____   Skill: Money

Draw a line to match the coin to the correct amount.

50¢

5¢

1¢

10¢

25¢

© Carson-Dellosa CD-3746   92

Answer Key

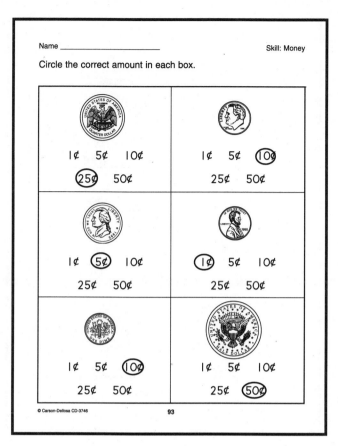

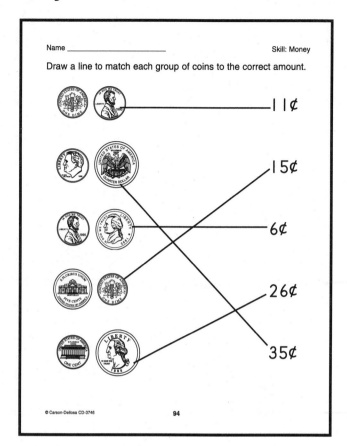

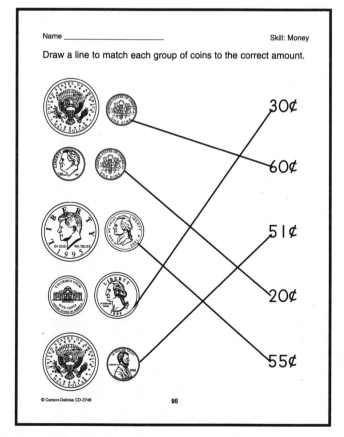

Answer Key

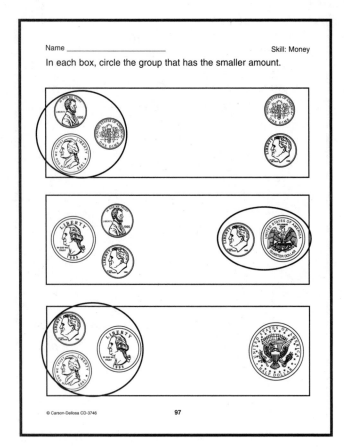

Name _____   Skill: Money

In each box, circle the group that has the smaller amount.

Name _____   Skill: Money

In each box, write the correct amount in the blank.

45¢   11¢

16¢   40¢

75¢   51¢

1 + 1	1 + 2	1 + 3	1 + 4
1 + 5	1 + 6	1 + 7	1 + 8
1 + 9	2 + 2	2 + 3	2 + 4
2 + 5	2 + 6	2 + 7	2 + 8

5   4   3   2

9   8   7   6

6   5   4   10

10   9   8   7

2 + 9	3 + 3	3 + 4	3 + 5
3 + 6	3 + 7	3 + 8	3 + 9
4 + 4	4 + 5	4 + 6	4 + 7
4 + 8	4 + 9	5 + 5	5 + 6

8 7 6 11

12 11 10 9

11 10 9 8

11 10 13 12

5 + 7	5 + 8	5 + 9	6 + 6
6 + 7	6 + 8	6 + 9	7 + 7
7 + 8	7 + 9	8 + 8	8 + 9
9 + 9	1 − 1	2 − 1	2 − 2

12 14 13 12

14 15 14 13

17 16 16 15

0 1 0 18

$\begin{array}{r} 3 \\ -\ 1 \\ \hline \end{array}$	$\begin{array}{r} 3 \\ -\ 2 \\ \hline \end{array}$	$\begin{array}{r} 3 \\ -\ 3 \\ \hline \end{array}$	$\begin{array}{r} 4 \\ -\ 1 \\ \hline \end{array}$
$\begin{array}{r} 4 \\ -\ 2 \\ \hline \end{array}$	$\begin{array}{r} 4 \\ -\ 3 \\ \hline \end{array}$	$\begin{array}{r} 4 \\ -\ 4 \\ \hline \end{array}$	$\begin{array}{r} 5 \\ -\ 1 \\ \hline \end{array}$
$\begin{array}{r} 5 \\ -\ 2 \\ \hline \end{array}$	$\begin{array}{r} 5 \\ -\ 3 \\ \hline \end{array}$	$\begin{array}{r} 5 \\ -\ 4 \\ \hline \end{array}$	$\begin{array}{r} 5 \\ -\ 5 \\ \hline \end{array}$
$\begin{array}{r} 6 \\ -\ 1 \\ \hline \end{array}$	$\begin{array}{r} 6 \\ -\ 2 \\ \hline \end{array}$	$\begin{array}{r} 6 \\ -\ 3 \\ \hline \end{array}$	$\begin{array}{r} 6 \\ -\ 4 \\ \hline \end{array}$

3 0 1 2

4 0 1 2

0 1 2 3

2 3 4 5

6 − 5	6 − 6	7 − 1	7 − 2
7 − 3	7 − 4	7 − 5	7 − 6
7 − 7	8 − 1	8 − 2	8 − 3
8 − 4	8 − 5	8 − 6	8 − 7

5 6 0 1

1 2 3 4

5 6 7 0

1 2 3 4

8 $-\ 8$	9 $-\ 1$	9 $-\ 2$	9 $-\ 3$
© CD-3746	© CD-3746	© CD-3746	© CD-3746
9 $-\ 4$	9 $-\ 5$	9 $-\ 6$	9 $-\ 7$
© CD-3746	© CD-3746	© CD-3746	© CD-3746
9 $-\ 8$	9 $-\ 9$	10 $-\ 0$	
© CD-3746	© CD-3746	© CD-3746	© CD-3746
© CD-3746	© CD-3746	© CD-3746	© CD-3746

© CD-3746

6 7 8 0

2 3 4 5

50¢ 10 0 1

1¢ 5¢ 10¢ 25¢